RISE

SE

SURVIVING
THE FIGHT OF MY LIFE

PAIGE VANZANT

hachette
BOOKS

NEW YORK BOSTON

TRIGGER WARNING

This book contains sensitive material that could be disturbing or triggering for anyone who has previously been the victim of sexual assault, sexual violence, rape, or sexual abuse.

If you are feeling triggered, the resources referred to on this page are generally held to be reputable and helpful:

The Rape, Abuse & Incest National Network (RAINN)
rainn.org

RAINN National Sexual Assault Hotline
1-800-656-HOPE

National Suicide Prevention Lifeline
1-800-273-TALK

AUTHOR'S NOTE

This is my story and my truth.

It's not an easy one to tell.

To avoid unnecessarily identifying anyone in particular,

I have taken the liberty of changing some of the names

of the characters that appear in the book.

Hachette Books

Hachette Book Group
1290 Avenue of the Americas, New York, NY 10104
hachettebooks.com

twitter.com/hachettebooks

First Edition: April 2018

Hachette Books is a division of Hachette Book Group, Inc. The Hachette Books name
and logo are trademarks of Hachette Book Group, Inc.

The publisher is not responsible for websites (or their content) that are not owned by the publisher.

The Hachette Speakers Bureau provides a wide range of authors for speaking events.
To find out more, go to www.hachettespeakersbureau.com or call (866) 376-6591.

Photo Credits: Pages 4, 100-101: Tim VanBergen; pages 18 and 62: Paige VanZant; page 112:
Reebok; page 150: Zuffa LLC via Getty Images, provided by the UFC.

Rise
Words and Music by Danny Gokey, Josh Bronleewe and Benji Cowart.
Copyright © 2016 BMG Platinum Songs, Creative Heart Publishing, Wordspring Music, LLC,
Word Music, LLC and Howiecowie Publishing
All Rights for BMG Platinum Songs and Creative Heart Publishing Administered by
BMG Rights Management (US) LLC
All Rights for Wordspring Music, LLC Administered by W.B.M. Music Corp
All Rights for Word Music, LLC and Howiecowie Publishing Administered by WB Music Corp.
All Rights Reserved Used by Permission.
Reprinted by Permission of Hal Leonard LLC

Note: due to the sensitive nature of the content that follows, some names have been changed.

Print book interior design by Timothy Shaner, NightandDayDesign.biz

Library of Congress Control Number: 2017959715
ISBNs: 978-0-316-47226-5 (hardcover); 978-0-316-47227-2 (ebook),

Printed in the United States of America

LSC-C

10 9 8 7 6 5 4 3 2 1

TO MY PAST:

You should have killed me

When you had the chance.

INTROD

I could rattle off a list of injuries that I have endured—every rip, gash, cut, slit, stitch, crack, sprain, pull, twist, and tear that's somehow or another wreaked havoc on my body. That said, I'm not scared of getting hurt. I see injuries as occupational hazards, expected and unavoidable. Consequences that simply come with the territory.

But there's one piece of hurt that I have always kept buried.

A pain that I keep locked deep inside, and that for all these years has been consciously untold, even to my family; a pain that undeniably affected my physical body, but did its real damage to my soul. This one was more than an injury—it was a spiritual wound. The scarring kind.

The special blend of darkness that I experienced turned into some kind of wildfire, snapping and ferocious, a wicked force that took on a life of itself. And once it took, it ravaged. It developed. It evolved with me as I grew up. It clung to me and became an undercurrent throughout the course of my life, a shadow that always slithered beside me, maniacally laughing while it tried to pave my path with darkness.

But I didn't write this book to talk about how life knocked me out. I wrote it to tell the story of how I chose to rise.

I wrote it to purge the murky junk and shadows from my past, so that I can keep propelling forward, toward the light.

I wrote it as a testament to the fact that your deepest pain can become your highest purpose.

I wrote it for all the women who got knocked down and came up swinging.

But mostly I wrote it for the girls who are still lying on the ground right now wondering how they're going to make it.

This is the story of how I chose to *rise*.

I'm not AFRAID.
I was born
TO DO THIS.

—Joan of Arc

TOMBOY IN A TUTU

It's raining, which makes me want to be outside even more. Because rain means mud. And mud means fun. I love it when my sneakers get all caked up with soil, layers of dry, dinosaur-like mud from hours and days and weeks and years of riding my bike through that spongy, gravelly mess, under low-hanging gray Oregon skies that keep the earth beneath my wheels perfectly, consistently moist. Every day, I cruise through the streets on my BMX, up hills and across the farmlands with my hair whipping at my neck, into the joyful surrender of that innocent, happy, earthy filth. I race against the boys, and very often win. They both love and hate me for it. But mostly they respect me for it.

Mom will be bummed if I'm not home by sundown, but I just want to keep riding my bike like a comet through the night. I want to ride until I can see all the stars winking at me, until I can't breathe, until my knees stop working. I want to ride faster than anyone else. I want to be outside, to feel the air on my skin and move my body. But I holler to the guys that I gotta *jet*, pull a sharp right and head home because I really love my mom. Also, I know what she's got in the oven, and I'm not about to miss out on that. They all look at me funny as I ride off, not because I'm the only girl in the pack—they're used to that—but more so because I'm wearing a pink taffeta tutu, its layers flapping in the breeze like giant butterfly wings.

When I get home, the house is steamed cozy with the smell of my mother's signature tater tot casserole. Chester, my dog, who is basically my mom's third kid, greets me with a tackle and a facelick. My dad won't be home until everyone else is in bed, since he works nights. But Mom always makes enough for him to eat later, which I know he does with great pleasure, because I can usually hear the scraping on the casserole dish from my bedroom on nights when I'm up struggling to fall asleep. Our folks were kids themselves when they had my brother Stevie and me. They met at a hardware store in 1988 and proceeded to become quintessential high school sweethearts. Mom says I came into the world ten days early, mad as hell, ravenous and screaming my head off at every doctor and nurse around me. When her milk didn't come down fast enough, I'd get impatient and lash out, flailing my tiny arms and scratching up my whole face. I'm told that I was a scrapper since the beginning, a strong and determined newborn, keen on holding my head up right from day one.

Mom and Dad are great parents because they expose us to everything and they let us try everything. They don't tell us what to like; instead, they show us all the delights of the world as if they were on a menu at a restaurant. They let us pick what sounds good to us. From the grimy to the glamorous, be it indoor or outdoor, they love to see us dive into things, to get excited about our activities, to milk every hour of sunshine there is. They show up, facilitate, support, and encourage, often at the expense of their own plans and budget. They live for us. They encourage our curiosities. Instead of boundaries, they give us turbo boosts. We don't have a lot of money, but there's always good music playing and tasty food cooking in our house. Quality-versus-quantity type of people.

Dad is a control room operator at a paper mill in town. When he gets home after a long shift, he brings with him the musk of hard labor and pressed ink. He's a no-nonsense man, both direct with us *and* there for us. He's the kind of guy who works five to six hundred hours of overtime each year and never flinches, tough skinned and strict, a tinge of ferocity always set into his smile-less gaze. Machinelike in his ethic, Dad just powers through things. No matter what it is, he stares it down and quietly pounces. He doesn't mince words and has a low threshold for bullshit and weakness. My mom says my father has a condition called intermittent explosive disorder, which is essentially what it sounds like. The man has a short fuse. But I take his tough-love style with a grain of salt. People tend to tiptoe around him, but I prefer to rise to his challenges, to show him what I'm made of at every opportunity.

"I'm just gonna go ahead and assume you aced the hell out of it," he proclaims on days when he knows I've had a test, his way of instilling confidence. It's safe to say, he's my first-ever coach.

Mom is a dancer. She has that quintessential dancer carriage, all posture and lines. For a while she owned a dance studio called the Chehalem Valley Dance Academy, but she sold it when I was four years old to become a full-time stay-at-home mom. Thanks to her, dance has been in our life since the beginning, like a whole other language in which we were always fluent. In our household, dance isn't an extracurricular activity, it's an extension of being alive. It doesn't matter that we live in rural farmlands—or maybe *because* we live in rural farmlands—dance imbues our days with poetry and elegance. Ballet, jazz, tap, modern, hip-hop: whatever it is, being involved with it transports us elsewhere, shows us something else. I *love* to dance; it's been true since I was a toddler. I love the excitement that builds in the space of those two or three beats just before the song drops in. I love the freedom that comes with music, and the expression that comes with movement. I love how each song has its own path and how the body responds to certain sounds. I love pointing my toes so hard that my quads bulge up and cramp. I love knowing my steps so well that they're not even stored in my memory, but in my body. I love being so consumed by a dance that I forget where I am. I love the feeling of nailing it. I love how my muscles feel when they stretch and flex, every part of me coursing with the fire of being all in, the sound of the music egging me on.

My dad says I've also been wrestling since the age of two, which shouldn't come as such a surprise to him, because he was a die-hard wrestler himself in high school and college. My dad doesn't treat me like a precious little princess—he levels with me, he encourages scrappiness, and he measures his respect for me at any given moment based on my grit quotient. He's unkind, tough, and doesn't believe in positive affirmations. And yet I love the guy and implicitly trust him. Maybe he avoids the accolades as a way to push me to do even better. His way of making sure I don't go soft.

He likes hearing my accounts of the neighborhood boxing matches, in which I sometimes participate, casual backyard sparring with the local boys. We try to knock each other out, and the whole point is to see how many hits you can take and still stay on your feet. He doesn't worry about me being the only girl out there. On the contrary, he likes to hear the details of which gloves I wore, and if I made eye contact and whom I knocked out and how. One afternoon I come home with bloody knuckles and a victorious grin. Most dads would probably freak out at the sight of their daughter's injuries. Not my pop, though. He's got the heart of a Spartan.

"Let me see! Atta girl, way to rough 'em up," he says.

"You should see the other guy!" I say, forever eager to make him proud.

He loves everything about fighting: watching it, doing it, talking about it. It's in his hands and it's in his heart. When he watches fights at home, I can hear the crowd chanting in the background, sonic waves of human energy swirling around the performance and momentum of two fighters. My dad locks into the intensity of these fighters, his eyes keen on every move, every intention. It's like he's on the couch, but he's really on the mat. He should have been a fighter. That would have been his dream—and he would have been good. But like many of the fathers in Newberg, he had us young, and since his life quickly became about our needs, he had to sacrifice his own aspirations with hard labor to make sure we'd never have to walk away from an opportunity.

* * *

Our town is shaped like a bowl. The rich people live up top. We live at the bottom with all the farmers, where the mingled smells of cattle and fruit trees always hang in the air. Newberg is in western Oregon, near the Willamette River, less than an hour away from Portland. Even that close to a city, it remains a mostly rural town, settled in the nineteenth century by a fur trader and a bunch of Quakers, and surrounded by the quiet farmlands of Yamhill County.

We live on two acres of land by a river and a creek, near endless acres of rolling farmland and two national parks. We have a pond, too, which I like to think of as my own personal mud bath. I love slinging mud at my buddies and getting so soiled up with earth that the whites of my teeth pop when I smile. I love the carefree abandon of being dirty and not caring and drying up in the sun and falling asleep at night so fast and deep because I am so physically exhausted from running around outside all day. When I'm not on my bike or skateboard or boxing in someone's backyard, you might also find me up in one of the elaborate forts I build with some of the other kids in the woods. My muddy, messy, DIY, perfect dominion.

We're not farmers per se, but there have always been animals in our world. I definitely remember bottle-feeding a pair of baby goats that used to live with us when I was little. Hershey and Coco. I can still remember the expressions in their eyes, the velveteen softness of their coats, and the sweet looks they gave me as they chugged down their milk. We got Chester when I was six, and though I have never been one to play with dolls, I go out of my way to get Chester in outfits, especially hip-hop gear.

But favorite pets, livestock, fields, and pastures aside, when it comes down to it, there's nothing really here, in Newberg—rich or poor, up or bottom. I mean, it's calm and lush and green, and the sheets of trees and rolling hills are cool, but ultimately there's nothing really here. Which I guess is a good thing because it's always made me feel kind of antsy and active, hungry for something, like an adrenaline rush or some kind of action or adventure—or all of the above. Maybe the quiet vastness of the farmland makes me somehow want to compensate and fill myself up with life. That's how I feel, anyway. Full of life. High octane. Hungry. In refusal of boredom. Sometimes it feels like I came into this world packed with an extra battery.

I have so much built-in moxie that I really thrive in Mountain View Middle School. Science is my favorite subject, and Mr. Kaltwasser is an amazing teacher. I love how dynamic his class is. We do lab work, but we also garden and build rockets, which we get to explode. I'm intent on straight A's. If I don't get them, I sometimes cry. I also get mad if I'm not on time for school every day. It's because I'm a die-hard perfectionist. I love the thrill of competing, and I consider my classes just another arena for mastery.

But by the time I'm ten, I start to feel an itch. Maybe I'm starting to outgrow our town's humdrum, predictable rhythms, or maybe I'm just tired of the same old, same old. Either way, I start to crave a sense of *more*. I don't want to stay locked into a life of boundaries, I want to push my edges, I want to raise my bar. One particularly rainy afternoon, I'm in the car with Mom coming home from a dance practice, and a commercial comes on the radio.

"Do you think you have what it takes to be a Disney star?" the announcer asks, which to me sounds less like a question than an affirmation of some deeply known truth. "Have you always dreamt of being onstage or -screen?" the voice asks, this time one octave higher. The answer is a resounding yes, and it comes from the part of me that feels like I've been sitting in the waiting room of life. The ad is for John Robert Powers, a well-known modeling and talent agency that trains kids for Disney's pilot season in Los Angeles, a period of auditions during which the network casts all its shows. That night, I watch Miley Cyrus in one of her many colorful iterations on TV, and get hit with a mammoth revelation:

I don't want to watch what other people do—I want to be what other people watch.

"Honey, you've got enough talent in your left pinky alone to end up on any one of those shows," my mom says.

"You think so?" I ask, but the real question burning inside me is *How the hell can I accomplish that while I'm stuck here?* I need to be somewhere where lives don't just unfold haphazardly—I want to be where lives are built!

With Mom's help, I start taking regular classes at John Robert Powers, and immediately I feel right at home. The dance element is old hat to me, and the newer worlds of acting and modeling are fun to learn. I love playing improv games and being handed a set of circumstances that I suddenly have to bring to life. Now lines in scripts start to come alive for me as more than just words; I'm being compelled to weave them into realistic emotions, into actual scenes. Songs are deconstructed into pieces of music that I learn how to navigate with every part of my voice. I learn how to carry myself, how to breathe from my solar plexus, how to command attention, how to strike a pose. I learn how to smile with my eyes, I learn what "stage left" and "stage right" mean, and, most crucial of all, I learn how to really stand in the light.

I begin to wake up to the fact that there's a world beyond Newberg. I can taste it. It simmers beyond the blurry farmland horizons, flickering into the edges of my bright-light fantasies. A world where people are driven by a desire to excel. To perform at their peak. To crush it. A glamorous world in which women dance in high heels, talent and hard work pay off, and waking up for hair and makeup before sunrise is just part of the routine. The world I'm talking about is Hollywood. A bright, sunny world where peak performance is the name of the game. And that's the world I want.

The phone rings.

"Hello? Is Paige Sletten available, please?"

"Who's calling?" Mom asks.

"We're calling to let you know that Paige has been officially invited to participate in the Disney pilot season in Los Angeles. Will she be able to come?"

And don't ask me how, but I manage to convince my folks to let me have a shot at this. They agree to let me spend a span of four or five months in Los Angeles, where casting agencies and production houses will hold all kinds of auditions to cast up for all the new shows in the works. Mom, my brother and I pack our bags and move to a whole other state, where she will homeschool us. My dad stays back in Oregon; he's working, as always.

I am too young to realize how incredibly cool all this is of my parents. To give me a chance to follow a dream. To go after it. To let me have this moment. But that's just how my parents are: Tactically supportive. Facilitators. Ground-layers of opportunities. And unconditional in that quality.

Like me, my mom and dad grasp the fact that despite my having to drop out of school for several months, this endeavor could quickly become an opportunity. And like me, they understand something key: *we won't know unless we try.*

We base ourselves out of a Holiday Inn located in Burbank, a tiny room with twin beds, where the clutter of outfit changes, hair accessories, and textbooks quickly pile up. It's not the glitz and glamour of my fantasies, but right away, the giant sunny skies and cheerful pastels of Los Angeles make me feel happy. Its tall, skinny palm trees stand perfectly crooked in the sunsets, and there's a dry desert warmth crisp in the air. The whole experience is a nice respite from the drizzly, leaky skies of Oregon. Hoodies to flip-flops feels good, for a change.

Disney pilot season is like boot camp. Our mornings start at six o'clock sharp. Mom gets me fed and does my hair, and we go over the list of rounds for the day. We have a manager, Joan, who is basically my agent and drills us on all the open casting calls happening. Joan talks fast and moves even faster, as if each second of her day is part of some master plan. My mother drives me to each call, drops me off to do my thing, and drives around until I finish. I love the independence. On the way to my auditions, Mom loves to remind me about how when she first dropped me off at preschool, I asked her to leave me at the entrance because I wanted to walk in all by myself.

I wait in long lines alongside armies of other girls, coffee cups and makeup bags in hand, each one a soldier for the cause of her own glossy success. We are all simultaneously in it together and one another's opponents. There is as much tension as there is perfume in the air, but I douse myself in confidence and walk right in to everything. Right from the start, I'm amped. I feel like I'm home. I love the electricity of the planning and the silent intensity of the drive to each audition. Of course, I feel the pressure. But the nerves fuel me and transform into a fire in my belly that refuses to let up. I drink up the process like honey. I was made to do this.

Every casting person is different. Some greet me with warmth and impart a vote of confidence from the start. Others don't even really look at me. I'm just a name to tick on their long, lined yellow notepad. I walk into one audition, and the casting director herself is fifteen minutes late, and when she finally does walk into the room, a deafening silence comes in with her. Everyone seems terrified of this person, who moves her glasses to the very tip of her nose as she watches me deliver my lines. When I accidentally read the word "thorough" instead of "through," she stops me with a single loud clap and instructs me to take the whole thing from the top. I'm somewhat mortified, but I respect the perfectionism!

I make it a point to arrive at each audition with courage leading my way and fifteen minutes early. I make sure to smile with my eyes. I project my voice when speaking, and make each dance step as precise as a punctuation mark. I keep telling myself to honor the details. I walk away from each audition with my heart racing in my throat, with a certain emptiness that comes with not knowing when or if these people will ever think of me again. The whole experience is at once empowering and humbling.

After a few months of this, of lingering in greenrooms, memorizing lines, learning lyrics, waiting for phone calls that don't necessarily come, and praying for just one lucky break, the season is over, and it's time to go home. Some callbacks trickle in. I manage to get one national commercial for a mop, and I pull off a few runway shows and ad campaigns for Nike and Columbia Sportswear. But what really matters is that I get a taste of the hustle.

Back home in Oregon, the dancer in me is lit more than ever. The Disney scene and LA in general ignited even more motivation within me. I spend more time in my mom's old studio. I take all the classes: ballet, hip-hop, lyrical, jazz. But my favorite is jazz, because it has a real structure with exciting turns and unexpected jumps. I dance so much that I start competing, even choreographing some of my own pieces. To take it up a notch, I switch gears from my mom's studio and join other ones, such as MVP Dance Elite and Dance Vision. I become a Junior Blazer Dancer, too, which means I get to perform at Trail Blazer basketball games in Portland during halftime in front of thousands of people. There is really nothing quite like the energy of a massive crowd, their roar, their excitement, their singular focus on whatever is happening on the court, be it basketball or dance. Right from the start, I feel connected to the idea of performance, the grind of rehearsals, the sweat life, the mental part of having to memorize routines. Dance becomes the thing around which everything else happens.

When I perform at the Hollywood Connection, a dance convention and competition, I earn a gold medal for my solo. I win platinum, the highest award, at Star Power, which is another national dance competition, and take first place for my division. My folks, who don't have any extra funds to spare, especially now that my mom doesn't own the dance studio, somehow manage to scrounge up whatever money they can so that I can keep competing. In two months, I think they spent two grand on competition-related expenses, which was pretty much Dad's whole Christmas bonus. Mom even starts teaching private dance classes on the side to be able to afford a lot of these extra expenses. She takes it all very seriously. Luckily, I get to go to the Tremaine Dance Convention on a scholarship. Every win stokes the fire in me, pushes my personal bar even higher. Every leap forward makes me hungrier for even more.

ICED OUT

My mother and grandmother were both Newberg High cheerleaders, so I figure that having a third generation of cheerleaders could be really cool for our family history. Plus, I'm athletic and a dancer, so cheerleading is an obvious go-to. Games, fans, team morale, spirit, practice: the perfect constellation of variables to really kick off an awesome social life, which is going to be key when I start ninth grade in a few months. At the end of eighth grade, I try out for the squad with my friends Tammy, Jesse, Lisa, Laura, and Faye, the lot of us keen on proving ourselves. Making the team will be our calling card to being badasses in high school.

I'm not intimidated by the tryouts, because learning choreography is my middle name. I pick up the routines quickly, and I can tell that the coaches are trying to look neutral but are really impressed by me. Since I dance so much, I have stamina to spare, and I know how to use my facial expressions to make the routine pop even more. It feels like everything I have done in my life is somehow building to this very moment. I keep making the cut, moving from tier to tier, with fewer girls in each squad every time we move ahead. My buddy Tammy gets cut, and as she walks off the court, I can see her fighting back tears. After a few rounds of this, I learn that I make varsity, a feat I know often takes years to accomplish. In fact, I am the only freshman from my school to make varsity at all, which leaves me dizzy with emotions: proud, for managing to make the final cut, but also excited about the prospect of ninth grade turning into something really memorable.

But the start of the new school year brings with it a certain shift, an intensity that I didn't see coming. There are kids from all walks of life at my new school, children of farmers and winery heirs alike. I am enrolled in all AP and sophomore-level classes, which are a bit advanced, and in which I don't know any of my fellow students. My classes are made up of all new people, a total reshuffling of faces and familiarities. My old routines are shaken up, and in their place is a whole new mash-up of classes, criteria, and crowds. Thousands of pairs of new eyes size me up daily. Maybe they don't know what to make of me, this sporty-girly-brainy person. So each day is like walking into a new abyss. A place with no point of reference, no axis, no sounding board, no exchange. In ninth grade, I find myself suddenly on my own.

Even though I'm not in the same classes with my crew from middle school anymore, I still try to hang out with them during lunch or free periods, but the minute they found out about my making varsity, something seems to have shifted. I can tell Tammy feels slighted because she didn't make the team, and in an effort to salvage this relationship by not further upsetting her, I take down all my cheerleading posters and photos from the wall before she comes over to my house one afternoon to hang out. Why rub it in, right?

I start to realize that what began as us just naturally drifting apart, the way kids often do after transitioning into a different level of school, now feels like full-blown rejection. It's not distance that I feel from Tammy—it's straight-up animosity. She and her pack try to convince me to quit the team. I guess if they can't be on it, they feel I shouldn't be either, as some kind of gesture of solidarity. But that will never happen. They start to ice me out and really shrink into the distance, and every step I take forward moves them farther away. I know that I need to land somewhere socially this year, but I just can't tell where I belong.

I begin to feel an unfamiliar void. When I lean over in class to try to join in on the chitchat, Tammy talks over me, pretending my voice is inaudible. When they laugh about an inside joke, I am not privy to what it is. The first week I tell myself that this is all normal, that things just need a little bit of time to settle into place. I try to remember that humans are creatures of habit, and that once everyone gets used to the new rhythms of high school, we'll all pal around like old times. But by week four, I realize there are events I don't know about, social media groups I'm not on, and secret handshakes I don't get taught. And it becomes clear that no matter what, I am now officially on the outside of something.

There are no friends to be made on the cheerleading team itself either. In fact, much like Tammy and my old friends, the other cheerleaders clearly don't like me. It apparently took most of them years to get on the squad, and I made varsity on my first try. They hate that. Each day, I grapple with the irony of giving it my all and not doing as well to appease their concern. I learn our first routine so well that I'm able to perform it without one single mistake, and when I smile at Linda, one of my teammates, as if to say *Our squad is going to crush it*, she just cracks her neck, rolls her eyes, and looks the other way. Even though I am one of them, I'm simply not welcome into their world. They all seem to have it out for me, like they're looking for reasons to knock me down. They actually rat me out to the coach for letting a non-cheerleader girl—whom I saw crying in the hallway, and whom I wanted to console—wear the team jacket. For reasons that I cannot understand, they want me to fail.

I can't talk to my coach about my concerns, as her own daughter is on the team. But things get even weirder. For instance, I'm the smallest person on the team, which means—according to physics—I should technically be the "flyer" in the group. A flyer, in cheerleading, is the one who gets thrown up and caught as part of a routine. But the girls don't think I am worthy of being a flyer because of my level of seniority, which is nil. They want me to do my time, to earn it. So I resign myself to standing at the back in our formations, and I regularly get pummeled by double my weight. One hundred and fifty pounds of quivering she-flesh, flying directly at my face.

When I leave practice, I can feel their scowls on my back, the lot of them standing there with their bellies overly sucked in and their hips cocked, none of them even trying to hide the fact that they're gossiping about me. They not only don't like me, they don't like the very essence of me. They don't want me on their team. But it also feels like they don't even want me on this planet. Something somehow got lit in their minds about who I am or what I represent. How do these things start? How do people develop these narratives or notions about other human beings and feel suddenly entitled to perpetuate them for the purpose of harm? I try to pinpoint what it is about me that they're so mad at or against; I try to be the best possible teammate. But no matter what I do or say or try, it's already rotten with them. They want nothing to do with me. Their togetherness itself is a blatant power over me, and yet they stay away from me like I'm the plague. Their rejection is active. The gates are closed. "So, you're a dancer. Big fucking whoop," I hear Laura, one of the other flyers, mutter one day.

No matter how many times I chew it over in my mind, I can't grasp the "how" of it. How could I go from being so excited about life and happy to this . . . sad and confused loner? My focus in class is even starting to shift. I used to be an avid note taker. Now I find myself staring out the window more, daydreaming about the life I thought I was going to have in high school, and wondering how things spiraled into my current reality. When I come home, I'm not the bubbly, zealous kid I used to be, and instead of rattling off all the awesome adventures of the day, I sit in my room quietly and chisel away at my homework, feeling frustrated about the day that just passed and nervous about the one that's coming next. I hate feeling like a victim, but right now I can't escape it. My parents tell me to have faith, to give things time. They're used to a daughter who aces everything, so they probably think I will eventually have things under control.

"Stop being a pussy," Dad says, without a hint of reserve. He's not much of a talker, but when he has something to say, the words come like bullets. "And we both know giving up is not an option." I know this should comfort me, but I still can't make any sense of it. What is it about me that these kids hate so much?

At night, I listen to the wind looping around our house, and I force myself to sleep because I know that each new day is a chance to make things better somehow. To meet new people. To try to make some new friends. To shuffle the cards and see what else the deck has to offer. I look my loneliness in the eye, and I make a pact with myself to keep trying. But in the mornings, the fear of the new day creeps on me. The fear of not knowing what to expect or that I'll make a mistake. Sometimes the day is so lonely that it gets to like four p.m. and I realize I haven't actually spoken a single word to another human being.

I am in all these great advanced classes—but I have no classmates my own age. The solitude weighs on me. The invisibility. I know I am friendly and fun loving, but I can't seem to shake the disregard from the girls on the team. Our whole mission as a group is to foster good spirit—*cheer*—but there is absolutely nothing cheerful or good spirited about the way I feel around these people. It feels strange to have to plaster a smile on my face when we perform, but performing is the only thing I have to hold on to, so I keep doing it.

I try to focus on schoolwork to hold me up because the loneliness starts to feel like a growing tornado that constantly swirls all around me, locking me in. But the competitor in me knows the game isn't over. This is still a transitional time, and nothing great happens fast. I have to do my best to stay open and optimistic, and have faith that something good is just around the corner. There have got to be some avenues I have not yet explored.

I pour all my feelings into the cheerleading routines, my limbs stretching, my heart racing, the sweat pouring. One afternoon after practice while I'm cooling down, Ivan comes over to me.

"Nice moves, kid," he says. He's a formidable young man. The rumor around school is that he's already earned a full-ride scholarship.

"Thanks!" I respond, unaccustomed to compliments here.

"You're really good, brah," he says, which makes me laugh. Something about the way he refers to me as "brah" reminds me that I am—and always have been—a tomboy, and that maybe I should rely more on that sensibility to mobilize my social life.

"Thanks, brah," I respond playfully, pleased with what feels like a micromoment of actual progress.

Ivan now smiles at me sometimes between classes, and asks me how I am. He even invites me to lunch with a group of the other jocks, and a few times a week we drive off-campus to Taco Bell. For the most part, it feels all right, if a little new (for lack of a better word) in some ways. On one of our drives to lunch off-campus, while I sit in the passenger seat of Ivan's friend's car, I see a tiny little plastic bag with what appears to be talcum powder. But I know it isn't talcum powder.

"When you gonna sell that, brah?" Ivan asks his friend.

"I don't know, man. Maybe I just won't," the friend responds with a husky giggle and a coy smirk, and he peeks at me in the rearview mirror. I have never seen hard drugs before. Sure, kids in Oregon smoke their fair share of weed, but this is a whole new can of worms. This does not sit well with me, but what can I do? It's none of my business, really, and it's not like they offered me any. *Nobody's perfect*, I think. *And welcome to high school.*

Sports is a huge deal in Newberg, and each win is celebrated by not just the school, but the whole town itself. Athletes and jocks are basically our local celebrities, so this new bit of socializing with Ivan and his friends feels like a lifeline to me, and I grab it to keep from sinking any further.

KILLED ALIVE

"Hey," Linda says softly one fall afternoon when I'm changing in the locker room after practice. Since I have gotten used to my teammates ignoring me, at first it doesn't even cross my mind that she's talking to *me*. "I said 'hey,'" she repeats, this time putting her face directly in front of mine, her head cocked to one side, her feathered side-bangs hairsprayed into place.

"Oh . . . hey," I say, confused, but also intrigued, and I fumble around in my locker to try to seem calm.

"So . . . there's this thing we're all going to." Some of the other girls in the locker room are listening intently but keep their distance.

"Oh yeah?" I ask, trying to keep it cool. But it feels like my heart is beating in my neck.

"Yup. On Halloween after the game. And we want you to come." She speaks with her arms crossed over her chest, her gum smacking inside her mouth like a drum.

"OK, sure!" I say, trying to sound both friendly and casual—but not too much in either direction. Maybe they're warming up. The school year is just starting, right? "Just let me know when and where." I'm grateful for the moment and already trying to figure out what I am going to wear.

Wow! It's actually starting to happen, I think. I knew it would all come together. The question is, why now? Maybe Ivan told them that I'm not so bad after all. Maybe they're starting to appreciate having me on the team. Maybe now that they see the guys being friendly with me, they are softening up. It doesn't even matter. The fact that they want me to come to the party is all I need right now. Later in the day, they even agree to let me be the flyer for that game, so that's confirmation that things must be on the up and up.

"So, yeah, like, just come to the school parking lot after the game on the thirty-first. We'll all leave together from here," Linda says, gesturing toward the other cheerleaders. In that moment, I want to throw my arms around this girl and hug her with all my might; I want to thank her for making me feel included.

I spend more time getting myself ready for the event than I care to admit, and in the car on the way to the high school I touch up my lip gloss and smooth down my hair at least ten times each. I feel equal parts excited and nervous, the latter of which shows up as a light coat of sweat on the palms of my hands. I turn up the music on the car radio.

"So, where do I drop you off?" my mom asks, pulling into the high school entrance.

"They said to meet in the parking lot," I reply, wiping clean a little streak of stray mascara from my lower eyelid, and checking the mirror one last time to make sure there's nothing in my teeth.

"You sure, honey? I don't see a single car," mom says, squinting her eyes.

"Yep. That's what they said," I answer, trying to camouflage any sense of creeping doubt. "I'm sure people will start to trickle in any minute now."

"All right, well here you are. Want me to wait, just in case?"

"Nah, they'll be here," I say, now feigning certainty. I turn the music down.

"OK. Well, why don't I just hang out for five or ten minutes? Can't hurt."

I shrug. Mom turns off the ignition and sits quietly. I look around a few times. I get out of the car and walk a lap across the lot. Maybe they hit some traffic; that must be it.

Twenty-eight whole minutes pass. Still nothing.

"Let's just go, Mom," I say, dejected, as I buckle my seat belt again.

"You sure you got the drop-off info right? We could always try to double-check, and I don't mind taking you wherever it is that you need to go. I gotta babysit your little cousin tonight, but not 'til much later."

"Nah. Let's just get out of here," I say, choking back tears. There's no one to call, nothing to double-check. I don't want my mom to even suspect what I already know—which is that I have been unequivocally pranked. Stood up. Lied to. *Dissed*. I feel confused, hurt, and enraged all at once. Being ignored was way better than being humiliated. Fuck those girls! Fuck Halloween. And fuck this whole situation.

On the drive back home, mom puts her hand on my arm. We both stay mostly quiet. We don't want to admit the obvious. Maybe if we don't talk about it, it will just dissipate like a rain cloud.

I silently close my bedroom door and cry into my pillow. I don't want my father to catch even a sliver of my weakness. They're both already so proud of my performance as the team flyer that day that I don't want to tarnish the one thing that feels good right now. But when I go online, I see that Linda and all the other girls are actually at a party, drinks in hands, having a fucking ball. Linda is wearing bunny ears and making a kissy face, while two of the other girls wink and throw peace signs. For a moment, I consider deleting my Facebook account. I fucking hate them. After a good cry, I pull myself together, take a good, long look in the mirror, and decide to snap out of it. Screw those girls and their dumb party.

And I guess the universe is on my side, because at around nine o'clock, I get a text message from Ivan. He says a bunch of the guys are going bowling, and he asks if I want to join. Perfect! Who needs those catty bitches? My mom isn't thrilled about me leaving the house so late, but I think she feels so bad for what happened earlier that she lets it slide. I wipe my makeup clean, tidy my hair, put on a happy face, and jump in the car with the guys when they pull up to my house.

We have a total blast, which shouldn't surprise me, because after all, *this is who I am.* I'm the girl who can hold her own with the guys. We eat mountains of fries and chase them down with icy Cokes, and the guys seem impressed every time it's my turn to go. When they drop me off at home again, I feel like a new person. *Sometimes all you need to do is open a different door,* I say to myself. Maybe I'm the kind of girl who does better with boys, and that's just all there is to it. At the end of the day, that's not a bad thing.

I feel relieved that the day is ending on a positive note, and after the emotional roller coaster of the last few hours, I'm pretty beat and ready for some sleep. But just as I'm brushing my teeth and getting myself ready for bed, I hear my phone buzzing again. It's another text message from Ivan. Huh. What could that be about?

Yo. That was fun, P.

Since it's Halloween, we decided to keep the party going.

A bunch of us hangin at my friend's house.

You in?

I smile to myself, feeling a sense of relief course through me. Relieved that people want me around, that I am thought of, that my presence means something. I start to write back, but I'm not entirely sure what to say. On the one hand, it's pretty late already (even if it is Halloween), and I really was just about to get into bed—but on the other hand, I don't want to fuck things up with

them. If they had so much fun with me that they are already calling back *on the very same night*, I must be doing something right!
Before I respond to the text, I check in with my mom and ask her
if I can go.

"Absolutely not," is her answer. "You were just out with them,
and it's already past midnight. No way."

Shit. "Come on, Mom!" I plead. "I'm really trying to make this
work! It's a Friday night! Please, can I?"

"No, honey. I'm sorry, but enough is enough. Don't you think
there's been plenty of excitement for one day? There's no reason to
overdo it. Your dad will freak out if you're not home by the time he
is, and besides, I can't drive you anyway. I have your baby cousin
here and no car seat, so you very well know I gotta stay put. End of
story. Get some sleep. Tomorrow's a new day."

I borderline scream something incomprehensible even to
myself and stomp down the hall to my room, where I slam the
door, and stew for a few moments in my own growing rage. She
knows I'm having a hard time. How could she not get why this is
important? It occurs to me that this is one of those moments when
I should take contrary action for my own sake; that right now,
maybe it's more important to think for myself than to temporarily
appease my mom for the "little miss perfect" title with which I've
held up. Also, it's Halloween, for the love of Jesus! I'm not gonna
just sit here while everything gets screwed up. No freaking way.
Not tonight. So, with a heart laced with panic, but a mind determined, I do the one thing that I have never once done—or even
thought of doing—ever before: I wait until she's asleep, and like a
stealth ninja, I sneak out of the house.

*   *   *

There's a crisp chill in the air as I walk to Ivan's friend's house, which is not far from where we live. Fallen leaves in rainbows of rust, gold, and brown crackle beneath my sneakers, and the candy-confetti remnants of the night's trick-or-treating activities also trail the streets. You can almost smell the sugar in the air. There are graveyard vignettes and skeletons dangling off doorways. Fake cobwebs made of stretched gauze wrap and droop on some of the mailboxes, and toothless pumpkins smile at me with a sinister look in their blank triangular eyes. I feel slightly guilty about defying my mom, but also relieved that she won't come after me, not with my baby cousin on her watch. Dad won't even know I'm gone. I may be doing the wrong thing as a daughter, but this loneliness is fucking killing me. *Sometimes you have to make sacrifices*, I keep telling myself.

I arrive to the address that Ivan gave me, where I expect to hear music, or at least the sound of talking or laughter. But when I ring the doorbell, I'm struck by how quiet things are. When the door opens, a waft of skunky-smelling weed smoke comes barreling out, and I quickly see that there aren't more than four people there, all of them guys.

"Hey," I say meekly, trying to make sense of the scene.

"Hey yourself," Ivan says, his eyeballs pink and his eyelids droopy. "Come on in, party's just getting started." His voice is low and sluggish. Maybe they are watching a movie or something, but it's clear to me that it's not a party—or at least not the kind of party I was expecting. I linger in the doorway for a few seconds, for a moment wondering if this is a good idea. Ivan looks at me and smiles. "Well?" he inquires, the door now creaking wide open. Screw it, I go in. What could be wrong with staying for half an hour? I decide to make the most of it and chill.

"Come on, this way," Ivan says, walking through the house in his socks, until we reach the back bedroom. Dub music is playing loudly, its trippy, loopy sounds riding a heavy bass line. They all look pretty stoned, sunken somehow, but they perk up when they see me walk in. One of them theatrically loads up a glass bong the size of a small person, lights it, and sucks in a mouthful of cloudy smoke so thick it's practically opaque. He holds it in until his face goes red, while the other guys cheer in approval. I don't smoke pot—never have—so I make every effort to steer clear of the smoke. Part of me starts to feel like I should just head back home and call it a night. After all, I gave it a chance, I came over, and now that I see it's just a bunch of dudes getting high in their shorts, I lose total interest in being there.

One of the other guys is holding a bottle of watermelon-flavored vodka, whose fermented sugary aroma mixes in the air with the dank stench of the freshly smoked marijuana.

"You drink before?" he asks me, while the others look on, their eyes only half open.

"Sure, I have," I respond, which is a blatant lie. I have never done any drugs or drank any alcohol. I've also never lied before just to fit in, but again, sacrifices must be made.

"Awesome. Then you'll love what we have in store for you on this very special Halloween," he says, assembling a little arsenal of shot glasses on a makeshift tray of textbooks, filling each one to the brim with the foul-smelling pink booze. The rest of the guys mumble and chuckle unintelligible words, and even though I am in there with them, I suddenly start to feel left out. "Bottoms up, Paige," he says, handing me a little glass. I don't want to drink it, but I don't want to be rude, either. I am in high school after all; I'm going to come across alcohol at some point. May as well be right now. I close my eyes, take a deep breath, and take a sip of the stuff, its rank flavor pungent in my throat. "Oh, come on now, Paige. You can do better than that, can't ya?" he says, with a hand motion signaling me to finish the whole shot. I look around for Ivan's gaze, since he's the one I know best out of all of them. They're all smiley and droopy eyed, watching to see what I'm going to do next.

"Drink up, Paige. We're celebrating," Ivan says, with enough friendliness in his tone that I reluctantly allow myself to oblige. I quickly chug the rest of the shot, after which I start coughing wildly, my eyes burning, and my throat now on fire. The guys laugh and clap. "Give her another one," someone says. He's plucking the strings of a ukulele with his pinky fingernail, which he keeps longer than the rest of his nails. "She just needs some practice." I feel queasy from the first one, and I definitely don't want any more, but before I can even decline, another shot glass is shoved right under my nose. "You can do it, you're a tough girl. You're one of us now," Ivan says, rooting for me (I think). I drink the second one, the sugary poison in my larynx like lightning, and again cough like a beast, this time my eyes tearing up a bit, my breath momentarily sucked away. More laughter. More claps. Another round of bong hits ripped. Another mammoth cloud of smoke blurring the unfolding reality inside this horrible little room.

"It's getting late—I think I should start heading home," I try to say, the smell of my own breath now physically revolting me.

"Home? Are you kidding?" one of them says. "You just got here, girl. You don't wanna be a party pooper, do ya?" Everyone else laughs and continues to drink and smoke. I am handed yet another glass, after which the guys all start chanting, "Chug it! Chug it! Chug it!" Their voices are eager and loud. I don't want to drink anymore, but I am in deep now, and I don't have a better option. I can't go home now reeking of this booze, on top of already having sneaked out. That's a double whammy that I am not prepared to face. So I drink the shot, vowing to myself that it will be the last one, knowing that I am in the throes of a peer pressure so heavy that it feels inescapable. When I empty the glass and slam it down, the guys howl with delight. I try to speak again, to say that I am leaving for real this time, but the words start to melt in my mouth. My thoughts become kaleidoscopic, and a wave of nausea comes at me like a typhoon. I don't even have the energy to puke. All I can do is sit there, my weight sinking deeper and deeper into the ugly carpet beneath me. Someone turns the music up, and suddenly the room starts to spin. Glassfuls of liquor keep getting shoved in my face, and one of the guys even tilts my head back to make sure I drink everything up. I have somehow completely lost control of the situation without understanding how it has happened. I lose agency over myself, but my mind is present, watching. Wasn't I just out bowling with these people? What in God's name is happening?

With my eyes, I can't see clearly anymore, and everything starts to blur into a fog. The rest of the guys are drinking, too, but none of them seem to be struggling the way I am. Something is clearly wrong here. I try to lift my arm to take my phone out so I can call someone for help, but one of the guys plucks it right out of my hand and turns it off. "We don't need that, do we?" I hear him say, his voice now sounding warped, muffled, and distant, like a record played on too slow a speed. My body starts to go numb, even though my awareness is still very much in the room. It soon becomes evident to me that I can't move my arms or legs, and my whole body feels like the weight of a hundred sandbags, like I'm stuck in a tank full of thick, viscous molasses.

Time starts to feel like a series of haphazard strobe lights, slivers, and shards of scenes like half dreams flashing in and out of focus. Now I'm lying on my back on a bare mattress that's on the floor, looking up at the ceiling, where hulking shadows move around me in ways I don't quite understand. I'm being held down, my shoulders pinned into submission. Someone is taking my pants off, and then my underwear. Someone is playing the guitar, its normally sweet sounds the soundtrack of a living nightmare.

There is a bustle around me, and then on me, a living massiveness holding me down. There is a constant pressure on my wrists and thighs. I feel a hot breath close to my face, and perspiration on my skin, which I can tell isn't my own. Suddenly my insides feel abnormally compressed, and there's a tightness and a painful pressure within me, inside me, that almost takes my breath away. No one seems worried about my being conscious or not. It's their ritual, I'm just a prop.

"It's my turn," says another voice, drunk with equal parts substances and a disconcerting eagerness. They move me around. They change my position. I fail each time I try to resist, my limbs like wet cement on my body, my brain a heavy fog. I am awake and conscious, but my body feels dead. I know what is happening but can do nothing to stop it. I have no voice or choice but to submit and pray that it ends soon. I can think of only one thing to do right now: I try to fall asleep. I hear laughter. I keep smelling weed. And the hideous sound of the ukulele keeps going, just like these guys. I am paralyzed but somehow my mind goes into prayer. I pray not to die, to figure out some kind of escape. But they drain me of dignity, over and over again, until I am nothing but a pile of my own bones. I have glimpses of their greasy acne faces, like monsters. Their different body odors pungent with every breath I take. There's a line of Axe body spray bottles on the nightstand where the TV sits, and I try to fix my gaze on them, because I need some kind of anchor.

I try to open one eye, but it feels like the whole room tilts and swirls into another dimension, pouring my consciousness from one place to another in a stream of thick tar. My body feels weighted, and an ominous wave of nausea starts to roll in on me like a storm in the distance. I try to sit upright, but my balance drips away from me, and my vision goes double. The inside of my mouth tastes like a wad of cotton that's been soaked in witch hazel, and my eyes feel puffy and zipped closed. My body hurts from the inside, with the unfamiliar heaviness of an ache whose exact location I cannot pinpoint, but which I can feel rippling through even—and especially—the nonphysical parts of me. My insides pulse with the pain of something that feels at once horrifyingly present and suddenly absent, like a pressure and a theft. And from the waist down, I feel like one giant bruise. I'm wearing a man's T-shirt and nothing else. Despite the specter of unfamiliarity and the fuzziness of the details, I know where I am and that I am badly hurt. I search desperately for my clothes, to no avail. I don't have time to make sense of the situation—I have to get the hell out of here.

My phone. I spot it on the floor on the other side of the room. I scramble off the mattress and crawl on my knees to it, and by a miracle of God, there is one bar of battery left on it. Twenty-seven missed calls and sixty-five texts from my mom. She must think I am dead or missing, because when she texts me the words "are you safe," as per our mutually agreed-on code for safety protocol, I'm supposed to answer back with the number "4" to confirm that I am. But now the words "are you safe????" appear in distress-laden repetition on the screen of my phone. I text her instantly, miraculously recalling just enough detail to let her know where I am.

4!!!!!!

come pick me up.

i'm at the yellow house at the end of the cul-de-sac.

there's a dented minivan parked outside.

Clutching my phone, I crawl out of the room on my hands and knees, terrified. I try to pull as much of the T-shirt as possible over myself. The stale smell of smoke and sweat hangs in my nose, and my exhales are laced with the nasty aftermath of cheap vodka. With every inch of pale blue carpet that I manage to traverse, I resist the urge to vomit. I make it to the kitchen, where the four boys are sitting around eating bowls of sugary cereal, crunching with open mouths. I sit still and wonder how I can get by without them seeing me. They look as if it were the most normal Saturday morning in the world.

"We thought you were dead" is how I am greeted after they notice me on the floor. I look around frantically, and they begin to laugh. But it's a laugh tinged with a new sense of panic, which makes me realize that they truly are surprised—and perhaps even terrified—to see that I am still alive. Are they really this fucking inhuman that this whole time they have been considering the possibility of having killed me? Is this an episode of *The Twilight Zone*?

Where the fuck are my clothes? I think, trying to drown out the obnoxious sound of their crunching and laughter and manic hungover energy. These guys are fucking pigs. *I have to get the hell out of here—I don't even care about my clothes.* I begin to crawl so fast that my elbows start to chafe raw. Ivan shoots up and tries to block my path, but a jolt of new terror courses through my body in the form of adrenaline and I manage to get all the way to the front door, which I open with shaking hands. I slither out like an animal, and right away see my mother's silver Honda Civic parked outside. *Thank God.* She got my text and reacted fast enough. They won't dare come after me now. A massive feeling of relief eclipses all the fear percolating within.

I stand up and limp my way to the car, my knees shaking, hoping to look less panicked than I am. I can feel that my body hurts but my fight-or-flight mechanisms are mobilizing me. I don't dare look back to see if anyone has followed me. I shoot forward steadily and manage to get myself into the passenger seat of my mother's car. I am at once escaping from what I fear could be death and trying to act calm for her.

"What the hell happened to your clothes?" she screams, with a look in her eye that I have never before seen. She stares me up and down, baffled. This is not the daughter she knows—this is a beast in the aftermath of a mess that neither of us understands. She doesn't know whether to scream or smack me. This is unchartered territory for both of us.

"I threw up on them" is all I can think to say, my voice so hoarse it sounds like gravel. I can't explain to her what I don't comprehend myself.

"You stink," she shoots back, and I can tell she's beyond furious, but maybe also relieved to see me. "Why didn't you answer your phone?"

"My . . . my ringer was off," I slur, which is the only recourse on which I can lean as I try to sift through the jarring scenes of the previous night for myself. How can I possibly tell her what I think I remember? It all feels like slush in my brain right now. But I can feel my mom's wrath burning a hole in me.

"I thought we agreed you weren't going out last night," she says, and goes on to berate me for disobeying her, for disrespecting her, for being reckless, for scaring the life out of her, for forcing her to leave my baby cousin in someone else's care so that she could deal with me, for putting her in a bad position with my father, for letting her down—all of which would, under any other circumstance, upset me to no end. But her words sound muffled, distorted, and strung together. I can't tell where one sentence ends and a new one starts, the anger just rolling out at me in constant waves. I don't respond. I can't. I stare out the window blankly, at the front door of that yellow house, praying it doesn't open, praying its awful secrets don't come tumbling out.

"You're lucky I brought you your gymnastics clothes," she says, grabbing a plastic bag from the backseat and tossing it onto my bare lap. "If you think you get to skip tumbling practice just because you were stupid enough to get stinking wasted last night, you got another thing coming." Her voice is loud, her nostrils flare. I hear her, but the questions in my own mind take over, and I'm desperate for her to push the gas and drive off. Flashes of moments from the night come up and just as quickly disappear, like lines drawn through water. "I'm taking you home, first. You need a shower. And here's some gum, for the love of Christ. You smell like death." Death is right. It feels like I have been killed alive.

"I'm so sorry, Mom. I won't ever do anything like that again," I say, absorbing the fault, with tears streaming down my face, pooling into my open palms. What the hell am I going to do? *Tell her?* I can't. I can't tell her, because there are no words for it, and even if there are, I am not going to utter them, because those fuckers do not deserve it. Still, I try and try to remember the details, but I just can't catch anything concrete. All I know with certainty is that something terrible took place last night.

I stand in the shower, unaffected by the fact that the water temperature is freezing cold. I don't even bother to make it warmer, because I am numb to all sensation, unplugged from the very core of my nerves. Maybe the freezing-cold water is powerful enough to wash away the truth. Maybe the shock to my system will wipe it all away. Each time I try to replay everything in my mind, the scenes shuffle in and out of order faster than I can keep track, as if a magician with a deck of cards is making every effort to guilefully trick away any inkling of my understanding. I watch the icy water trickle down my legs, observing whatever is left of my innocence wash down the drain with it. There is blood between my legs, and I remember that my period is in fact due right around now. I watch the dark red swirl of blood centrifuge down into the shower drain, wondering if it's period blood or something else.

Mom drives me to my private tumbling class, where I'm slated to work on back springs and back tucks that day, the thought of which, in the throes of my still-nauseated state, makes my stomach turn, but I'm thankful for a solid point of focus. I try to keep it together and walk into practice as if the last twenty-four hours simply hadn't occurred. Also, since the class is private, it costs my folks $60 per hour, which is a lot of money and they've already paid up front. Mom gets out of the car and this time stays through the class, watching from the bleachers, biting her nails the whole time. I can feel her disapproval on my back. I surprise myself at practice, catching more air than usual, and showing zero fear of falling flat on my face. I almost wish I'd fall and shatter every bone in my body, because at least that would allow me to rebuild from scratch, to not feel myself as I am right now—broken.

When I wake up on Monday, my mind is caked with uncertainty, and every fiber of my body tells me not to go to school—a feeling that I swallow whole for the sake of my parents, whom I won't dare bring into this catastrophic blur. I tell myself that the more normal I act, the less abnormal everything will feel. It's a matter of hitting delete on that particular event and moving on with things. So I go through the motions of normalcy, feigning the rhythms of my routines, pretending to be a person.

BAD TO WORSE

Mom drops me off, and from the moment my sneakers touch the asphalt, I can feel my feet rejecting any motion forward, the weight of my whole body bearing down on the ground, an involuntary protest of mobility. I want to plant myself into this little piece of earth and not take a single step forward into reality. I want to lock myself into time. I still cannot make sense of the last forty-eight hours, so how will I be able to face the next twenty-four? The only clues in my possession are a throbbing in both my inner thighs and the feeling that someone has taken a rake to the inside of my lower abdomen. As an athlete and dancer, I have always had a certain amount of pride in being consciously connected to my physicality, to my anatomical awareness. But today there is a chasm of unknowing between me and my body, a void where my connectedness used to exist. And despite the aches and pains of tenderness that tug at various parts of my bones and muscles, I feel completely severed from myself.

I linger at the car, and Mom looks at me, both wistful and confused about my demeanor and unusual pace. For fear of upsetting her even more, I curl my lips into a shape that's meant to resemble a smile, hoist my bag up onto my shoulders, and force one foot to move in front of the other, fighting every urge to run back to her and weep.

Right away I see Ivan. He's holding court, as he does most mornings, at the picnic table in the main yard. Everyone knows he's strong, but today he looks perversely mammoth to me, with his chest puffed out way farther than the rest of his silhouette, and his knuckles protruding like thick knobs at the ends of his fists. His hair is freshly styled with gel, forced into a fake crisp submission, as if his having gone through the trouble of setting his hair, as if a neat little hairdo, could somehow hide the heartless beast that is so visible to me. He's enjoying a coffee and waves his arms in the air as he talks, the rest of the guys rapt, cackling along. Then I realize that they're all there, the four guys from last night, a soulless band of assholes. A fury rises in me. I want to scream, act out, go over and fuck them up. My anger grows, shoots up, and boomerangs right back at me—now I'm angry with myself. I suddenly despise myself for being naive, for being so stupid as to think that these assholes wanted to be my friends. I scamper off in the opposite direction. I don't dare go near them—I must lay low and remain invisible today. But just an hour or so later, while I'm taking a book from my locker, I hear someone scream behind my back, "Look! There she is—Paige *Slutton*."

Halloween decorations still linger in the corridors of the school, haunting me. The memory of what happened so shattered that its millions of shards feel impossible to gather. But even the high school principal is aware of the buzz that seems to hang like a black fog over my head, because I discover that the four boys from the night prior are being questioned by the school administration. Apparently, someone called the school anonymously and reported an incident in which I was involved. I don't know if it was one of the guys, one of the cheerleaders, a suspicious teacher, or someone else. But there is clearly some kind of story circulating, enough to get on the radar of the school staff, and while it appears that I am at the center of it, I don't exactly understand why. It's not that I am stupid—I know something bad happened, but the events of the night flicker in and out of focus. Part of me keeps trying to sort it out and the other part keeps pushing it away—it's like I'm both desperate and terrified to know the truth.

While I am in music class, I feel a tap on the shoulder, startling me out of my own lingering daze. It's Ivan, and he wants to have a word with me outside. He lies to the teacher and says that the principal wants to see me, and since Ivan is one of the more popular guys in school, he basically gets to do whatever he damn well pleases. The music teacher gives the nod of approval and we both quietly leave the room, the rest of the students following us with their eyes.

"Listen, Paige. They're interrogating all of us," he says out in the hall, with accusation in his voice. He looks around nervously to make sure no one is around, then he stares at me, pupil to pupil.

There is a line of sweat forming on his upper lip. "I can't have you messing with my scholarship."

I stare at him, waiting for more information that might shed light on the events that transpired. I take in the details of his face, searching for clues to help map out whatever has led to my disgrace. His skin is slick with the grease of pubescence in full swing, and his eyes are a blend of vitriol and menace. I try to seek some warmth in them, any little hint of what I thought used to be, but instead I receive cold steel. *He is not my friend*, is the only piece of certainty that I have right now.

"Look. They're going to call you in, too," he goes on. "They're gonna ask you a bunch of questions about what happened last night, and if you don't want your life to suck even more than it already does, you'll keep your mouth shut, you got it?"

I don't answer—not out of protest, but because I honestly don't know exactly what it is that I am supposed to keep hidden. That I hung out with them? That I got drunk and blacked out?

"Paige," he says, with the bravado of someone who is not here to negotiate. "There's nothing you can do. We already burned all your clothes, so there's no evidence of anything. You're shit out of luck. So you're going to go in there and say that you came over and ended up falling asleep on the couch. That's it. Simple. If you so much as say *anything* else, we're going to show everyone the video we made of you last night. And trust me, you *do not* want that to happen, you hear me?"

Now I nod yes. A video? It could ruin my life. I'm being blackmailed about something that I don't even fully comprehend, but the last thing I need right now is even more shame. So when I am finally called into the principal's office, I do what Ivan said and lie through my teeth. This lie feels more tolerable than whatever really happened, so I run with it, and I allow the truth to fester somewhere far away.

Paige *Slutton*. Now I get it. People have created this horrific version of my name, Paige Sletten, because there is a crazy rumor going around about me. And rumors, I quickly learn, are like living things, growing and morphing the more they are fed. Everyone is apparently saying that I slept with four guys on Halloween night. The rumor ripens and blossoms with such vigor that this narrative about me starts to usurp my actual identity. I am swallowed whole by this ever-evolving lie; a lie that oddly, in the deepest depths of me, somehow starts to feel true. The more I try to act normal, to carry on with the day-to-day of life, to focus on my schoolwork and cheerleading, the more the rumor rears its head, haunting me, taunting me—like a beast that takes pleasure from watching me squirm. No one in school speaks to me, and when they do, their words are laden with cruelty. "What's up, slut?" I hear as I make my way from class to class, the words come at me razor sharp, ripping through my dignity. How can I possibly be a slut if I've never even had a boyfriend? How can a virgin be a slut?

I try not to think about Halloween night, which is the only shield I have against it. It's not even denial—it's a rewind in time, in which I literally have to act as if the night didn't occur, like it's a blip in my personal history that I have to stamp out like an ember. In order to erase it from reality, I must obliterate it from my memory. I bury it so far deep that it may as well be oblivion. It didn't happen if I can't recall it. It didn't happen if I don't know its details. And just like the rumor, which takes on a life of itself, I start to believe my own lies: This horrific thing simply did not happen to me. Period. But even as I try to block out the truth, deep inside I feel my life in two parts: life before Halloween and after. I know that whatever happened that night flipped a switch in me, and that in some way I will never be the same.

At Thanksgiving, I'm at the table, but only physically. I can smell the cozy aromas of roast turkey and homemade stuffing. Everyone is chatting and giggling and happy to be together, people playing with the baby, the dogs eating scraps off the floor. But there is a frost in my soul that doesn't allow those happy sentiments anywhere near me, and I stare at the television, which is on but muted, and I question the purpose of my life.

"Yoo-hoo," says my aunt Cara, waving a hand in front of my face. "You with us?" I don't answer with words, but attempt some kind of nod. The real answer is no. I'd be thankful to disappear, is the truth.

One afternoon during a water polo game for which the squad cheers, someone a few rows behind me opens a bag of watermelon-flavored candy. The achingly sweet smell reaches my nostrils, and I suddenly feel so vile that I may just puke right there. It feels like a smell that has the power to wake a demon from the deepest pits of hell, and without even thinking, I get up and leave the bleachers midcheer and go straight for the toilet, where I vomit so much that my throat turns to fire. When I come back, I can feel that all color is sapped from my face. But instead of any compassion or even a "Hey, are you OK?" from anyone on my squad, I get eye rolls, whispers, and side-smirks. Somehow, I have become the villain here.

It feels like there are two of me, and they are very much at odds: there's the me who keeps mentally going back to the bare mattress to search for answers, who tries to turn back time, to have stayed home that day, to erase those awful faces from my memory. This me searches in vain, clawing like a dog furiously digging in the earth for his bone, to figure out any clue I could've missed that would have predicted the events of that night. But there is also the me who comes to school each day, pretending none of it ever happened, hell-bent on getting good grades, and who uses classwork as the one buoy to cling to in an otherwise merciless and overpowering sea of pure, unadulterated shit.

But being in school feels like living in purgatory. I try to keep a low profile in the corridor as I walk from class to class, but it doesn't stop some senior girls from slamming me into the walls and saying mockingly, "Whoops!" as they run away in delight. And sometimes they don't run at all and instead form a human fort around me, staring me down like wolves about to pounce, cornering me into submission. "You better watch your back, Slutton," one of them snarls, her teeth gritting, her brows arched into wrath. Her face is so close to mine that I can see the hardened clusters of blackheads on the sides of her nose. The rest of the girls seem fueled by her antagonism, curling their upper lips at me.

When they finally walk away, I feel like yelling out "Cowardly bitches!" but I don't dare draw any more attention to myself, and instead hide in the bathroom. I close and lock the door and slide down to the cold floor, where I shut my eyes and pray for it to stop.

I pray for these girls to leave me alone, to stop drawing attention to me, to stop attacking me. I pray for this crazy rumor to dissipate, that people will stop caring about it, that it will just fizzle like everything else does. I stay in the bathroom as long as I need to come back to myself, but panic is with me for the rest of the day.

Every day I receive venomous texts from numbers I don't recognize. In these messages, I am called a slut, a whore, a hoe, a hooker, a cunt, a stupid bitch, sometimes all at once. I am called ugly, retarded, crazy, and screwed up. I am told that I smell, that I'm an embarrassment, that I don't deserve shit. I am told to shut the fuck up, to crawl into a hole, to crawl back into my mother's womb even, and also to jump off a bridge. When I open my locker, sometimes I am met with crumpled pieces of paper that contain drawings of stick figures in sexual situations, the words "Paige Slutton" accompanying every illustration to make sure I know that the female figure is meant to be me. When I come home at the end of each day, there are often globs of saliva nested in my hair. One time I come home to streams of toilet paper all over our house and condoms hung from the trees like Christmas ornaments. My parents just think it's the neighborhood kids being pranksters and don't take it seriously—and I don't have the heart to tell them otherwise.

I could survive if the disdain simply held its course—but it deepens and worsens with every passing day until I feel like I want to die. It used to be that I just got the silent treatment from people, but now it feels like they literally want to see me go away. There's something about my presence that inspires a unique kind of hate in some of these kids—like they can't fathom me even being around.

One afternoon, as I'm walking from AP bio to lunch, something smacks me in the back of the head. I turn around to see what's happened, only to find that a plastic bag of stinking garbage has been hurled at me, and a gaggle of senior girls giggle and run down the hall, pleased with themselves. It feels like there is a game being played, in which whoever is most successful in assaulting me wins. If I try to fight back, it will only fuel their fire. If I tell on them, it will get worse. My only option is to ignore it all, but with each little attack, I shrivel into a darker and blurrier shadow of myself.

And it's one thing that the mean students are cruel beyond words—but even the ones who don't do anything stare and whisper, like I'm a newly unveiled freak at a sideshow. I begin to wonder: What if there really is a video of me out there that people have already seen?

I devise new routes in school to avoid assaults in the corridor. I show up to class as late as possible, and take the last desk all the way in the back, which also allows me to slip out before class ends, so I can walk freely—alone—down the halls. I use sunglasses and headphones to shield me, and I blare Eminem's "When I'm Gone" on repeat so loudly that his flow fills me and drowns out my life. I think about death as the one thing that could rid me of this pain. And the only thing that stops me from moving on this idea is the understanding that if I die, the pain won't actually end, it will transfer to my parents for life. I can't do that to them. And even though I try to ignore the call of death and dying, it leers at me, like a crooked, bony finger summoning me close, to the point

that I think not only of ending my own life, but also even fanta-
size about showing up to school with a shotgun and killing everyone in sight.

In classes, I'm a ghost. I walk into English lit one day and sit at
a desk, and right away the girl sitting next to me—clearly settled
in already, with her notebook and textbooks open and pencil in
hand—closes her books, gathers her things, stands up, and goes to
sit at another desk, several rows behind me, as if the very state of
proximity to me might render her inferior. I don't enter the cafete-
ria anymore during lunch, because the stares and the pointing are
far worse than the deafening silence that comes with sitting alone.
I take my lunch to the bathroom, my one safe space, and lock the
door behind me, both plagued by this and grateful for the solitude.

I catch a sliver of hope one day when a sweet kid named Mike
asks me out on a date. Finally. Someone nice. Something to do. A
welcome distraction. But as we're walking back to the parking lot
after the movies, we see that someone has spray-painted the word
"slut" all over his truck. "What the fuck!" he screams and never
calls or speaks to me again.

Even my very own brother seems to be buying into the hate. I
try to be friends with him, to slip into his world, but I get the sense
that he doesn't want to be burdened with my issues. "You're not
gonna ruin high school for me, too," he says, completely shutting
me out. I have no old friends, no cheerleader friends, and certainly
no guy friends. It's worse than having enemies—it's like not exist-
ing at all.

I juggle the concentric layers of all this bullshit against the
memories of Halloween night. These flickering images grow like

a super ivy in and around all my thoughts, wrapping me with never-ending tentacles, holding me all twisted up in place. It's like living in a straitjacket made of my own experience. The gauzed up, muffled, muted memory of whatever those stubble-faced monsters did to me tries to emerge in my consciousness like the dead rising from a nailed-up coffin, attacking any sense of peace, showing up even in my sleep. I am never safe, because these demons now live inside me—they have the controls. A girl who once believed in magic, miracles, dancing in fucking Disneyland, and had massive dreams, now doesn't even want a happy ending for herself. She wants to disappear.

My life becomes a series of hidings. I hide my grief at home, I hide my pain at school—and everywhere I go, I hide the truth. I cannot let the misery come home with me, because I don't want my parents to worry, or worse, get involved. They work so hard—I don't want to be a source of their stress. I also don't want to be the girl who needs her mommy to rescue her. That will only make everyone hate me more. And I can't afford even one more iota of hate in my life. But Mom knows me, and she must see that the light in me has dimmed. And as far as Dad goes, I don't dare let him in that I'm in pain. He wouldn't be able to process the fact that I am in emotional pain. It's not a language he speaks. He glares at me if I cast my eyes downward, which is his way of saying "I didn't raise suckers around me, so straighten up."

"Baby, you doin' OK?" Mom asks when I come home one day, my eyes sunken, my spirit crushed. I am doing far from OK. I want to die. I want to stop living. I want to never have to see those kids in school again. I want life back to the way it was. I want this feeling of panic and agony to go away already. And though I want to tell her everything, to rip open my hurt, to ask for her help, I swallow the lump in my throat, take a deep breath, and force a smile.

"Yeah. Just tired, that's all."

But I can't keep the charade up for much longer, because every day I crumble more, little bits of myself disappearing into this new version of me that even I don't recognize. The sadness takes a turn, and instead of just feeling the weight of the pain, I start to leak it out of me in streams of tears. I have to leave class and hide inside my trusted bathroom stall, where I can cry alone, where I can give voice to this misery. One day it hurts so bad that I call my mother from the bathroom, and she can barely hear the words between my sobs.

"Please come pick me up," I cry into the phone. "I can't do this anymore."

"What's the matter, honey? Talk to me. Are you hurt?" But she knows. She knows *me*, and she must know by now that something is terribly wrong. I've tried to camouflage it, I've tried to pretend, but she is my mother, she knows what I am made of, and she knows when I'm not whole. I don't answer and instead cry even harder. "Baby, don't move—I'll be right there."

And through this crack in my spirit, I start to let my parents in, because at this point, hiding my pain is like trying to conceal a broken limb. The days have started to take on a new rhythm. I go to school, I try to remain invisible, but words of ridicule or worse are hurled at me. It has just become the new normal. I break, privately, in the confines of the bathroom, where I surrender to the linoleum floor beneath me and slump into an anguish that feels as infinite as it does dismal. I call Mom, she comes to my rescue. She picks me up and we go for coffee and talk. I start to tell her more about the girls who hate me, about the physical violence in the corridors, about the venomous insults, about being the person whom everyone despises, about the piercing loneliness of my every day. The words come tumbling out faster than I know how to string them together, a typhoon of information that at once confounds and hurts her. I don't say a word about Halloween, because even an utterance of it might render it more real than I (and certainly she) am able to handle. I can see her mind working. She tries to hold strong for me, but her eyes go glossy and her chin starts to quiver.

"It's their loss," she says, blinking away tears. "And they're probably just jealous," she goes on, this time holding me close. "Screw those people anyway. You got us."

But the torture persists. My fellow classmates get meaner. It feels like the let's-hate-on-Paige thing has become a movement, something to join, a bandwagon to get on to somehow matter in the high school ecosystem. The cruelty is normalized. No one bats an eyelash and no one stops to care. The nastiness is pervasive, but even more upsetting is the lack of sensitivity from *anyone*. Even the teachers are blind to me. One day, in the bathroom stall, I cry, cry, and cry until there's a knock on the door.

"I'll be right out," I say, trying to compose myself, blowing my nose. I can't let anyone see me like this.

"Sweetie, are you all right?" It's my Spanish teacher, Carla. I open the door and she puts an arm around me, her brow furrowed with concern.

"Yeah, I'm OK," I say, but I'm clearly not, and it's obvious.

"If there is anything I can do to help, please let me know," she says seriously, which I appreciate. But this is bigger than her, and there's really nothing in the world she could do to make this right. What can she do? Call the entire student body's parents and tell on them? Make the cheerleaders like me? Go back in time and erase Halloween? I cry on her shoulder for a moment, grateful for the sliver of care, but when I leave the bathroom and walk back down the hall, the pain bubbles to the top, reclaiming every little piece of me.

I hear Mom and Dad talking outside my bedroom door one Sunday morning, their voices muffled, the conversation laced with an undercurrent of distress. The volume goes up and down and soon I can tell the conversation is about me. She confesses to him all the layers of my struggles, how I have been challenged at school, the bullying, the lack of friends. He listens quietly and I can practically feel his disappointment through the drywall. He's just not a touchy-feely guy, so this kind of business is simply not his ball of wax. If I had to guess, I would say he probably doesn't even know what to do with the information. After a few moments, my door swings open again, and there's Dad, equal parts melancholy and ready to pounce.

"You're telling me you don't stand up for yourself?" he shouts, but it's less a question than a declaration of disbelief.

Throughout the morning, he paces around the living room trying to think up a way to help me through this, because he can't fathom the thought of my weakness. This is a man who sees the world in the context of two types of people: those who handle shit and those who don't. Even though he never explicitly says he's proud, I know he has always seen me as someone strong. The thought of anything other than that crushes me.

A few hours later, a police officer shows up at our house, at the behest of my father, who is not a time waster. "My kid's getting aggressively bullied," is what I hear him say. I know his heart is in the right place, but I also know there's no way he can truly understand the path I've been on.

"Here's my advice to you, young lady," the cop says, his thumbs hooked onto the front of his pants. "You get back to school tomorrow, and you figure out who's the biggest, meanest one of those gals. Now, the next time you see her comin' around your way, you take a big ol' textbook and you hurl that thing right at her face," he says, without a single word of hyperbole. My dad's eyes light up at the sound of this counsel, and my mom shakes her head and lets out a whispered "Sweet Jesus Christ."

"Listen to the officer," Dad chimes in. "And don't even bother coming home until you've properly fucked up one of those good-for-nothings and taught 'em not to mess with you. I want to see blood." That's Dad, fierce, proud, a warrior to the core. I wish I could absorb that ferocity, really take it in, and do as I am told. But the fire in me is down to nothing, and the mere thought of creating any additional tension scares me. I can't imagine being violent toward another person—I feel so battered with fear that I can barely make a fist.

When I do go to school the next day, I clutch my books close to my chest. When I see Linda, I look down at my calculus book, which is the thickest one I have, and I grip it so hard that my knuckles go white. I replay the cop's words in my mind—*Hurl that thing right at her face*—but I can't muster the wherewithal to do it, and I sink back into my pain.

And her eyes TELL A STORY,

Of anger and pain,

You think that she's happy,

But just LOOK AGAIN,

And the scars of her past,

HIDDEN under her clothes,

Are a road map to places,

THAT NOBODY KNOWS...

—Unknown

TO HEAL A WOUND, RIP IT OPEN

Dad comes home earlier than usual one day. I hear a door slam and then the weight of his body slump like a sack into one of the dining chairs. I'm not used to seeing him in the house at this hour since he works nights, so I come downstairs to investigate and find him with elbows on the table, cradling his head in his hands, his eyes mournfully closed. Mom makes him a cup of coffee but doesn't say a word when she sees me. He sighs a loud exhale. Something isn't right.

"I guess people just don't read newspapers anymore," he finally says, lifting his head. "It's over." He sighs again, taking off his hat and gently lays it on the table like a flower on a grave. It becomes evident to both Mom and me that my father has been laid off.

"It's like the grim reaper came in. They let a hundred of us go in one swoop," he tells us, his eyes landing on the pile of bills where the mail usually sits. We moved into this new house less than three months ago, and our new mortgage is at least double what Dad used to pay. The air in the kitchen suddenly thickens with questions.

"We'll figure something out," is all Mom says. Her voice is warm with encouragement, but her face is another story.

"I'm not sure what my next move should be," Dad says, in a rare moment of vulnerability. "I guess I'll start searching around town for another job like everybody else. Hell, I may even have to look around for something somewhere else."

I know the very last thing they want to do is move anywhere else—it's why they bought this bigger house, so that we could plant our roots even deeper here. Our town is practically etched into their DNA. They were born in the same hospital, even delivered by the same nurse. They were married in the Newberg church, and they have never left their county, a voluntary confinement that fuels who they are. Leaving Newberg is like leaving themselves.

Without Dad's steady paycheck, our family starts to lose its worth, and the energy at home turns nervous and sullen. Dad sits at the kitchen table punching numbers into calculators and making phone calls with a put-on cheerful voice. He clears his throat before each one, takes a swig of coffee, his leg shaking like a motor under the table the whole time he talks. He starts to look for work at Portland General Electric, but they're not hiring, so he needs a plan C, and quick. But despite not finishing college, my father is very intelligent, and he's keen on getting our family back on track. He starts to read up on gas turbines, realizing that the energy sector has more of a future than anything in printing, which he knows is a slowly dying field. His days become a flurry of emails, endless research, and an incredible amount of pacing. Every now and again, he goes out on an interview, and he comes home even more distressed and disgruntled than he left. But one thing is for sure: the man does not stop.

After desperately digging around for opportunities all over the West Coast, he learns of an opening in Reno, Nevada, at an energy plant. The pay won't be much at first, but it's a foot in the door of an industry that's poised for a long game, and Dad is ready to shift gears and turn our luck around. Since the gig starts immediately, he must first relocate to Reno on his own. He drives there and stays for the whole workweek, then drives back to spend the weekends in Oregon with us. In the meantime, Mom is desperate to stay here. She picks up several different part-time jobs to make it happen. She works mornings as a crossing guard, then she takes on a few hours at a day care, then afternoons as a lunch lady, then back for the afternoon crossing guard shift, and after all that she still finds the energy to teach dance classes at the Sherwood Dance Academy.

"Mom, I'm dead serious," I say to her one night after one of her string of shifts. Her eyes are tired, her hands dry and rough; she's massaging a cramp out of her left calf. "Why don't we just move to Reno with Dad? What's holding us here?"

She looks up from the casserole pan she's scrubbing, trying to work something out in her mind. "I guess we could always sell this place, or rent it out," she says, surprising me and probably herself.

"Yes! We could just start over. *I* could start over, Mom," I say, the tears pooling in my lower lids.

She puts down the dish and brings me in close and I can feel her heart beating. We stand there together in the pain of so many different emotions. "I know, baby," she says, surveying the room around us with a stinging nostalgia, while her tears plop one at a time onto the top of my head.

Mom is crushed. And maybe even a little in denial that we're going to move. She reluctantly holds a massive garage sale for us to shed most of our things, stores a bunch of our special stuff in a barn, and gives our whole living room set to my aunt. My parents try to sell the new house, to no avail, so they find a way to rent it out to a local college, which is a perfect way for us to earn some monthly income, especially now that we're officially going to move.

I can tell she's struggling with the idea of relocating, but she's made peace with it, thinking about how good it will be for me. Because each day my fragility has become more evident. I feel like a thin piece of glass, always at the threshold of a shattering. On one of the days when she picks me up after I've suffered another private panic attack in the school bathroom, we're in the car and I'm heaving and weeping into the palms of my hands. I gasp for air between each sob, trying to cling to life, but desperate to leave it. I tell my mother that I want to die. She stops the car.

"Paige," she says looking me straight in the eye, her own filled with tears that she tries to conceal. "That's not an option."

"I can't take it anymore!" These words shout from the deepest parts of my pain.

"I have an idea," she says, shaking. "Let's change your name."

"Mom, I'm the problem—not my name!" I scream, frustrated.

"Stop for a second and think about this. What if we legally change your name so that once we move to Reno you get a clean slate? A chance to start fresh as someone completely new?" The air stands still, and we both linger in the silence of her suggestion. This never occurred to me, that I could start fresh, *that I could really start fresh*. I think about it some more. If I change my name, I really might have another chance—in a new town, on social media, and in my own mind. No more "Slutton." One hundred percent total newness.

My grandpa isn't thrilled; after all, it is our family name, and why on earth would anyone feel the need to change her name? But not even my sweet grandpa can dissuade me from shifting into this newness, and when Mom drives me to the government office to make it so, I rejoice in the prospect of this exciting rebirth. In fact, when Mom and I sit at the kitchen table one day brainstorming, she starts rattling names off like we're trying to name a newborn baby.

"What about Paige Summers?" I say, and she crinkles her nose.

"What about Paige VanZant?" she says, her eyes lit up.

Bingo! I can feel the hairs on my arm stand up, and a sudden chill passes through my body, as if with the discovery of that name I've somehow struck a deal with my destiny.

"Paige VanZant!" I scream, trying it on for size.

"So, young lady, why is it that you feel the need to change your name?" the judge asks from across a hulking mahogany desk. He's got thick glasses on, through which he sizes me up as I contemplate my answer. I try not to fidget with my hands while I look for the words.

"I want to change my name, Your Honor, because 'Sletten,' um, sounds like 'slut,' Your Honor, and it's making my life very difficult in school." I try to sound as composed as possible. Mom puts a hand on my arm and looks right at the judge.

"I see," the judge says, adjusting the glasses and scribbling a note.

"I just want to have a shot at being happy, Your Honor," I go on. "I need to, Your Honor." He looks at my mother and then at me again, the tenderness between us palpable.

"Well, let's call this day one of your being happy then," the judge says, and he signs the document that renders my name change official. "I wish you all the luck in the world, Ms. Paige VanZant," he says with a playful emphasis on the "VanZant," my new name, a word that may seem like nothing to most people, but to me in this moment feels loaded with possibility, and even more so, salvation.

I scrape by the rest of the school year, knowing—praying— that Newberg will soon be a speck in my past, and that I'll be able to rid myself of all this bullshit once and for all. Each day in that building with those people feels like death by a thousand paper cuts. I'm not able to keep a 4.0 average like I used to, but I manage to wrap up the year with decent-enough grades.

I'm drinking now. Cheap vodka mostly. Not because I like it, but because it helps me fade. Also because Joley and Emma, two senior girls who start semitalking to me, like to take shots after school, and I'm hanging on to whatever I can. They buy it with fake IDs, and convince me that drinking after school is awesome. Since they are the only two people who give me the time of day, I follow suit. They also convince me to ditch school one day. They encourage me to snag my parents' Suburban and drive us to my grandparents' beach house, where we guzzle booze and talk smack. I don't particularly even like these girls, but I allow myself to slip into their unruliness, to surrender to the dark. Fuck it, I don't care. The world is nasty to me, so I'm going to be just as nasty back.

"What the hell is wrong with you!" my dad screams, the wheels of his truck screeching hard onto the beach house's driveway just after he's called. We were sloppy and the neighbors called my folks to tell them what was going on. Joley and Emma scamper off, drunk and terrified, leaving me alone with my parents, who stare wide-eyed and heartbroken at the nearly empty vodka bottles that litter the floor. This is not the daughter they know, not by a long shot, so I can't tell what they're feeling more, anger or disbelief. But my misery has turned into Teflon, and not even their disdain has the power to shake me. I move through my life with a new kind of numbness, an indifference that starts to pluck out my dignity one judgment call at a time.

When summer arrives, we pack our five-bedroom house and load up the car, and I sit in the back seat, watching our now ex-home shrink smaller and smaller in the rearview mirror. *Never going to miss this shit*, I think as Newberg whizzes by me into the past, without so much as a shred of nostalgia tugging at me. I hate this place, I hate who I have become here. And as we drive away I begin to pray. I pray because as I watch my hometown blur into a history that I hope I can forget, I can still feel the presence of the demons within me—hissing into my consciousness, whispering miseries into my brain. It doesn't matter that we're leaving, going to a whole new state, because just as our car pulls onto the highway, I can feel that these demons defy geographical rules, and like toxic vapors, they swirl in the very air that I breathe.

Reno, Nevada—the biggest little city in the world. That's its tagline, anyway, but for us this quirky desert town with a stubborn blaze of sunshine feels more like Times Square with a panoramic Sierra Nevada backdrop, the massive crystalline Lake Tahoe acts as our very own local pool. You would think this would be a welcome change for my mom, but for the first few weeks all she does is cry. She doesn't know what to do with herself, and she's obviously worried about me. She fears the new town and new school could also mean new problems.

"Please just try to remember how much my life sucked in Newberg," I remind her. Sometimes, I use the words "kill myself" to really make the point.

And on the one hand, Reno does feel like a fresh start; but on the flip side I am still grounded for months over the beach house incident. My dad is still outraged over it, in disbelief of the fact that I would (a) hang out with those girls and (b) let them exploit me that way.

"Don't you see? They used you," he says. And as for Mom, she just can't handle the alcohol part and wants her sweet daughter back.

I know I should feel bad about this transgression, but there are too many other emotions happening inside me, so the guilt becomes dwarfed. The depression is like this thick cloud, a fog really, that blurs the importance of anything else in my life. Nothing matters anymore. Not grades, not cheerleading, not friends, not even family. I have officially given up on caring—even when it comes to my parents. As I sit cooped up in my new bedroom, my mind is a flurry of deeper questions: *Why am I still so down? What the fuck is wrong with me? Who do I want to be? Where do I start?* And the one question that lurks like a hungry shark in brackish waters: *How do I erase the past?*

There's also the matter of our new lifestyle. Gone is the rolling green and the dewy mornings. It's all strip malls and dry heat now. And gone are the days of endless space and ample square footage, because instead of the five-bedroom house that we were used to in Newberg, we now live in a two-bedroom apartment. My parents don't let me hang anything up on my bedroom walls, because we're renting, so there is this feeling that we're between lives somehow. The blank walls stare back at me but offer nothing. It feels clinical and devoid. Money is so tight that we don't even buy a television or a computer. Although I am not allowed to do much, my folks do let me use the pool, gym, and spa in the building, which is new for us, since we've never lived in an apartment complex where amenities are a thing. They also buy me a goldfish, which I name Bruce. For now, he and my dog, Chester, are pretty much my whole world.

I didn't bring much to Reno—but I definitely have my social anxiety with me. In tenth grade at Reed High School, I self-impose two rules: no dancing and no cheerleading. If I'm here to re-create myself, I have to start from scratch. Nothing that resembles the past, nothing that requires swarms of girls, nothing that's going to trigger those memories. The trouble is that I am at a loss, and I have no idea what to do, where to place my focus. So I mostly just linger and sulk. I'm happy to be gone from Newberg—but I'm not happy, per se.

"You can't just sit around all day hiding in your room," Dad says, a consummate hater of inertia. "Find something to do. Find something to put your heart into." He starts listing off ideas of activities for me to try. "Tennis. Basketball. Baseball. Boxing. Running cross-country—"

"Yeah, why not?" I say, faking vigor.

"Atta girl, that's the spirit—why not try something new?" He's pleased to see some effort. I don't want to add to his stress; he's got enough going on with his new job as the newest employee of a power plant, for which he's still on trial. He's got three months to prove that he's worth his paycheck, so we all walk on eggshells around him and try to keep any drama to a minimum. It doesn't help that funds are tight, with all the moving costs.

So I quietly join the cross-country team, mostly to appease Dad. My heart isn't in it, but it does feel good to move my body again, and I try to rally some semblance of motivation in the face of my overpowering lethargy, a physical heaviness that's new to me and that I can't seem to lose. If nothing else, running starts to shake the cobwebs off a bit. It throws me into rhythmic meditation and allows me—if only for a few brief moments—to replace my inner monologue with sheer physical output. It feels good to be in my body again. At one practice, the coach shows up with team jackets for everyone to wear. I'm mostly indifferent to the whole thing at first, until she hands me mine. It's black with gold accents and tapers on the torso. Then I turn it around to look at the back, only to discover my name VANZANT embroidered in giant capitals, covering the width of my shoulders. Coach paid for it herself, knowing that $150 would be too much for my family right now. The gesture moves me, catching me completely off guard. I marvel at how amazing it feels when people show that they give a shit, even just a tiny bit. I put on the jacket and stand with my back to the mirror in the bathroom, and for a half of a fraction of a second, I see the faintest little streak of light.

"Hey—Paige, right?" someone says while I'm sitting alone in the parking lot, waiting for my mom to pick me up.

"Yup," I say, slightly startled as I turn around to see a boy I recognize but don't particularly know. I am unaccustomed to any attention at this point, so I feel a layer of sweat building at my temples and on my palms. Fighting through a thick layer of anxiety, I quietly say, "And you are?"

"Alan. Nice to meet you." He stretches out his hand, which feels warm and soft in my grip. He has a smiley expression and he makes direct eye contact. It seems like besides my family, no one has looked me in the eye in ages, so this sudden gesture of intimacy feels novel. His face is sunshine. He sits down next to me, unsolicited. I pretend to be reading one of my books.

"Anything interesting?"

"Nah. Just passing the time."

"Wanna pass the time at Port of Subs? I'm starving."

"Now?"

"Why not? Life is short," he says, his smile electric. I don't answer for a moment, the last thing I want is a boyfriend, but there's something about him that feels safe. I quickly text my mom.

Don't come get me

Gonna take the bus

Meeting a friend

Love you

"All right, why not," I say, standing up, gathering my things. Right away, Alan offers to carry my books, which is the kind of thing I thought happened only in the movies. We start walking down a busy street, and he moves himself to the other side of me, over to the traffic side, which I can't help but read as yet another sign of subtle chivalry. He smiles softly, as if to say, *That's just how I roll.* We sit at the Port of Subs and order sandwiches too big to finish in one sitting, and sip on enormous cups of Sprite. The common denominator through all of Alan's behavior is the honeyed quality of his smile, effortless and ever present, like he came to the world clearly knowing his MO: to be happy. He doesn't interrupt me when I talk, and if he does, he immediately notices and apologizes for it. He says "please" when he asks me to pass him another napkin, and when he listens, his eyes blink a lot. His simplistic joy is contagious, and while we chat, I feel my own smile—which has been out of practice—now soften into my face.

"So, where you from?" he asks, which I know is a perfectly natural question for a new person to ask another. But my trauma, hell-bent on never looking back, speaks for me.

"I'm a citizen of the world," I say, pleased with my enigmatic answer, which also somehow resonates with me.

Alan slurps on his Sprite and lets out a little laugh. "I like that," he says, raising his eyes to meet mine.

Alan is my first-ever boyfriend, which is markedly different from having friends who are boys. With Alan, I am introduced to the world of affection, to the idea of tenderness. I am shown courtesy. I am given compliments. For some reason, he is able to see through my sadness into the core of me. He sees the truth beneath my standoffish exterior and he wants in. His warmth is a much-needed medicine, like a balm for my soul. Neither of us has a car, so we spend our time walking from place to place under a fat Reno sun, chatting about everything, learning little details of one another's lives. Sometimes he shows up with fresh flowers, other times he writes me sweet cards. He doesn't push me to say or do anything that doesn't feel right, and he seems content to just hang out and get to know me, with the occasional kiss, which are sweet and innocent. I can feel myself starting to soften when I'm with him, layers of my anxiety melting into comfort. Sometimes I want to tell him everything, but I always catch my tongue, remembering that words are like truth stamps that have the power to make things real. And I am not ready to face the reality of my past. So instead I relish the sweetness of his breezy companionship, the warmth of his chest, the softness of his earlobe, the shape of his shoulders, the way he says my name.

I'm feeling so much better than I have in a long time and I want to soak in my new feelings and never think of Newberg again. I want to keep gliding into the future, stamp out the past with each new experience here. And with every new happy moment, I do manage to slink farther away.

But even during the easiest, loveliest moments, when I think it's impossible to go backward, when life feels like it's at last taking me somewhere good, when the prospect of love and romance feels too good to be interrupted, the beast of my past shows its fangs again, reminding me that it still lurks close by. One day, I receive a text message from a number I don't recognize.

hey loser

we know you left because you're pregnant

now you're just a pregnant slut

The cruelty of the message claws through any sense of peace I have managed to achieve. My mind goes into overdrive: Who sent this? Why would they? What the fuck is this story? How did one stupid Halloween night in stupid Newberg turn into my everlasting disgrace? Why the fuck is this thing still following me?

I erase the message right away. I don't tell anyone about it. It starts to sink in that Newberg is a shadow that will slink behind me wherever I go. And the fear of never being able to sever myself from it will be my lifelong punishment, like a karmic penalty. Maybe I really do deserve this. Maybe it is the price I am destined to pay for sneaking out that night when Mom had clearly said no. Maybe this is what I get for choosing the wrong friends. Maybe every soul has a script before it's born into the world, and maybe there will never be anything I can do to change the fact that this is my story.

The beast of my past laughs when I entertain these thoughts and continues to wrestle with me, victorious as it eats away more of me, day and night, shrinking the essence of me down to a speck. I stifle all of it—the crippling emotions and even the news of the text message. I won't ruin Reno for my parents by sharing it with them, and I won't ruin myself for Alan by letting him in. This pain belongs to me, it's a tattoo on my existence.

I wish I could talk to my parents, to bring them into the truth. But I just can't. My mom is already struggling with the move, and I'm terrified of what Dad will think or do when he realizes that his daughter is nothing but a sulking, worthless Slutton. Instead, I start to drink even more alcohol—vodka, whiskey sours, tequila— which helps incrementally to keep the demon at bay. I don't even drink to get drunk, I drink to fall asleep, and if it were up to me, I would happily just stay asleep. Alan thinks "I'm going through something," but he doesn't push. Then even more hate texts start to appear.

hey loser

you should just kill yourself already

I should ignore the messages, change my phone number, block the number, anything to stop this heinous and unpredictable onslaught. Why am I allowing this to happen? Why don't I just tell someone already? But the words of that last message stay with me, like little prickles all over my skin. These words—"kill yourself already"—at once terrify and seduce me. I try to keep up with normal life, like cross-country, school events, and time with Alan, and do everything I can to avoid staying alone. I act like everything is normal, smile when he talks to me, and say nothing of my private hell. I hold on to the sweet moments with him as if just the act of being with him somehow undoes all the bullshit from my past. I use my hours with him as a shield—he keeps me safe from everything, including myself.

But wherever I go, panic breathes down my neck. When Mom drops me off at a football game one day, she drives off and I stand on the sidewalk trying to move forward, to simply walk into the venue on my own. But my legs go soft beneath me, and I start to hyperventilate. I'm dizzy and nauseated, and I start having chest pains. I feel terrified, agonized. I might just drop dead right here. I am physically unable to move from that spot. All I can manage to do is pull out my asthma inhaler and quickly call Mom. She drives back, shocked to see that I have not moved even a centimeter from the spot where she left me.

"Why don't you go in?" she asks, rolling the window down. By the look on her face, I must not look too good.

"I can't," I whisper.

"What do you mean, 'You can't'? Get in there. You're a grown-ass girl."

"I physically cannot. I can't move. Please help me."

With a gasp, Mom quickly gets me in the car. I know she can feel what I feel—I'm like a ticking bomb.

I try to hold on tight to Alan, to force more smiles. I try to act as if I'm OK, to pretend I am the cheerful girlfriend. But the beast hovers, dangling the memories like eerie marionettes right in front of my face. Sometimes it feels like I have one foot rooted in progress and healing, and the other one shackled firmly to the past, like a patch of quicksand slowly swallowing me, while tiny moments of hope try but fail to rescue me. Alan starts to see that it's something more than just a phase, that something is deeply wrong, but I don't yet have the heart to fully let him in. I try to kiss him back when he brings his face close to mine, to wrap my arms around his neck when he holds my waist. I allow him to spoon me when we lay around after school, but I want to scream when I feel his hot breath on my shoulder. The physical closeness feels oppressive, a heaviness that forces me to pull away. I wince. I resist. I tense up at the beast cackling just around the corner. The closer Alan gets to me physically, the closer I get to the story of my body.

It gets worse when October rolls around, and I start seeing Halloween decorations throughout the neighborhood, all those crooked pumpkin smiles and blank scarecrow stares. Candy corn served in cheap plastic pumpkin buckets at the front of every bank and store. Witch faces and skulls on the fronts of doors. The memories start to flood my consciousness, and the scenes from my living nightmare become all I can think about. It's like I am possessed, and no matter how hard I try to distract myself from the remembrance, to tell myself it's stupid, like oil in water, the truth always ascends to the top. The pain, which at first slowly nibbled at my mind with its sharp little teeth, now rips massive chunks from my sanity. Now it's not just my mind that feels overtaken—it's my whole being. Every fiber of my body, every single one of my cells, becomes consumed with a dull, gray toxicity, which keeps darkening with every second to the point where everything I see, feel, say, hear, and touch turns ugly. No matter what life offers, I will always be anchored to the truth of what happened to me. Nothing I ever do, nothing I ever feel, can sever me from my own history. I will always be that girl. There is no point to my life. There is only suffering. The backdrop to all my thoughts is a graveyard.

I can't take it anymore. I can't go on pretending that I am normal, that things are OK, that I even want to be alive. All I have is hell every single moment of every day. I need relief. I need to free myself from the constancy of this pain. No one should have to suffer this way. No one should have to fake her way through life.

I sneak into my parents' bathroom one night when they're out; I don't have a plan in place, but I am like a fire now, snapping wildly and out to burn without rationale. My actions are coming from a place beyond logic, from the dark place in me that is ready to stand in the jaws of destruction.

I am driven by sheer desperation, by something beyond myself. My sense of right and wrong is no more. There is no morality. There is only survival, which, ironically, can come only by dying. I open the mirrored medicine cabinet and eyeball every single bottle of medication I see lining the shelves. I don't know what anything really is. I land on a giant Costco-size bottle of Advil and take it in both hands. I shake it to gauge how many pills are inside—it feels mostly full. The words "pain reliever" stand out to me, they are lit up like the neon signs, and without thinking I take off the lid and stand there facing myself. I look at the reflection and I see two of me: the me who used to drink up the days, roll around in the sun, dance with her whole heart, the serious, no-nonsense athlete, the scrappy, smiley girl who loved to kick around in the mud. But the other me is more prominent, the me with dark circles beneath her eyes and the hole in her soul, the one who stopped caring about herself, much less anything else in her life, the one who feels irrelevant, invisible, and damaged from inside. Maybe this me is who I have become. Maybe that's just how some people evolve. That is the me who went into the bathroom and opened this cabinet. If I don't act fast, I'll lose my nerve, so without another moment of haste I dump all the pills onto the palm of my hand. I stare down the pile of liquid-gel capsules, their greenish-blue translucence somehow fluorescent to me now. It occurs to me that this might be the very last color I ever see. I close my eyes, unconsciously doing a thirty-second inventory of my life. I feel for my mom and dad; I can't imagine what this will do to them, but the pain tramples the concern. It wipes it clean. *I'm not good to anyone if I don't care about life*, I say to myself, a final testimony. I open the faucet and start swallowing huge batches of pills, following each batch with a giant chug of water, surprising myself with how fast they go down. I do four or five rounds of this until I have swallowed every single pill in the bottle. Chester is asleep in my parents' room. The house is completely quiet and still, except for an air conditioner quietly humming.

I wake up in the shower, covered in chunks of brown, pill-laden vomit. Chester is barking maniacally. I try to unravel things but I can't remember anything. My brain suspended somewhere between fury and relief. It feels like I have been asleep for two weeks. My body feels heavy and achy, and it's hard to keep a single thought straight. Thank God my parents are still at work, so I find my legs beneath me again, scrub myself clean, wipe up the puke, get rid of the empty Advil bottle, and go back to pretending that I have the power to prevail.

But the truth of my misery always makes itself known, like one of those trick birthday candles that you think has been blown out. The pain sneaks up out of nowhere, forcing my hand. So I continue to seduce death in my own private way, to tempt the darkness, to walk this dangerous line, especially when the house is empty. Dad keeps a gun at home for security; he always has. Sometimes I find my way to it, as if I am visiting a naughty friend that I'm supposed to stay away from. I pick it up and allow myself the grim satisfaction of holding it in my hands, the cold steel refreshing against the heat of my palm. I like the weight of it, which feels somehow indicative of its potency. This is not a plastic bottle of headache medicine. I could just blow my brains out with this thing. The thought both delights and disturbs me. I don't want to die—but I don't want to live.

Mom knows. She may not know the extent of it, but she knows it's not good. Not because I address any of this directly with her, but because she finds things. Like the words "FUCK LIFE—I just want to die" scribbled in thick black magic marker on my bedpost.

And notes all over my room with lists of people whom I want to kill, and musings about the meaninglessness of life and the lure of death. She starts to hide all the pills. I know this because I keep seeking them out.

She forces me to see a counselor at the University of Reno. "If you don't see a therapist, I have no choice but to get your father involved," Mom threatens, knowing exactly which buttons to push with me. I want my dad as far from all this as possible. He's not one for sob stories. I'll have to see this doctor just to calm Mom down.

Dr. Marks has kind eyes and a warm, even voice. She sits quietly and listens, but I say nothing during the first session. I literally just sit there staring at the ornaments lined neatly on her desk. I should tell her. I should turn this nightmare inside out, but instead I sit in that frigid air-conditioned room and fidget with my hands, defiant. The second time Mom tries to take me, I run away from the house. I run as fast and as far as I can manage, running from my mom, from the therapist, but really from myself. I disappear for a good five hours, because the idea of counseling feels like pouring lemon juice and saltwater into a raw, open wound. I just can't do it. After several hours of this manic getaway, I reach an empty park. I'm exhausted to the point of physical pain. I sit by a maple tree for a moment and stare at the leaves, contemplating the life span of each one, wondering why some get to turn gold and others just rot into an ugly lifeless brown crumble. By the time Mom finds me, I am asleep on the ground like a homeless person.

I can't keep my feelings under wraps for much longer, and Alan sees it. I respond to questions with monosyllabic answers.

I stare off into space. I pull away. I don't comb my hair. I live in sweatpants. I stop smiling completely. I don't even fake them anymore. He tries all his usual sweet stuff with me, but I increase the distance. I no longer have anything to give him, and deep down I don't want to give him anything. Our conversations are reduced to him trying to pry words out of me.

I lie. I tell him that I am fine. That he should not worry, that nothing is wrong. But he isn't stupid. "Sweetie, you gotta talk to me," he pleads often. "I'm here for you," he says, sincere as can be. I *should* open up to him, *at least him*. But I don't even know where to start, how much to tell, if it's even safe to confide in him. Where does my sadness even truly begin? How do I tell a boy I care about what happened to me when I was fourteen? How do I even think about articulating that story? What words do I choose?

When I try to answer any of those questions, the shame bubbles up like a venomous froth, suffocating me. The rawness of the reality burns in my memory. The pain presses on me, the way those boys pressed on me on that ill night I was violated by four different men, the night my life turned into ash. But Alan's sweet eyes don't let up.

"You know you can talk to me about anything, right?" he asks one night when I'm particularly closed off and quiet.

"I know," I say, lying, because I *can't* talk to him about the awful thing that happened to me. Even if I did have the strength to tell him, how do I know it won't scare him off, or that he won't judge me? Or worse, tell someone else? But there's Alan: stroking my hair, rubbing my back, making me tea—even when I don't ask for any of it. He doesn't give up on me, he keeps trying. Gently urging me to open up, to trust him, to find a way to see a light at the end of whatever is going on.

His love is genuine, so much that it starts to crack me. Very slowly, one kiss and caress at a time, I allow the closeness to comfort me. And soon, his love feels powerful enough to start countering the hate from my past. It starts to feel like a healing agent. I wrap myself up in it and try to let its warmth comfort me. I try to reach back to that sunny place in myself, the self that was happy, alive, energized, and I allow that part of me to let Alan in. I let his love serve as a rope. And I grab on to the end of this rope, and slowly start to pull myself up, allowing myself to open, to tell him, to tell the truth about what happened to me on Halloween. It's the first time I ever speak those words aloud.

"I was raped."

Each utterance a hideous reliving, each word like a nail in my own coffin. Alan takes it all in, like he's drinking a foul-flavored syrup, and I can see the breadth of his compassion expanding more and more, and it envelops me like a sacred wingspan—he's my angel in this moment. He asks no questions and makes no comments. His eyes don't leave mine as I tell the story. He holds me as I speak, and this gesture grounds me into the now, and for the first time since that awful thing happened, I feel untethered to death.

Driving back to Oregon feels like a death wish itself. The farmland pastures, which at one point in my life gave me a sense of calm and openness, now make my skin crawl with their incessantness. The lush, damp greenery used to be my playground, my happy place—but now it's the backdrop to the desolation that broke me. As we get closer to Newberg, I can feel my jaw go tight and the pressure build at the sides of my head. *What have I done?*

"You good?" Alan asks, one hand on the wheel and the other firmly gripping my hand.

"I don't know," I answer, knowing full well that I am nothing close to good. I want to tell him to turn the car around, to forget this whole thing. I want to tell him that I made the whole thing up just to get attention, that it's a giant lie. But the tears falling into my lap tell a different story, so he knows already, and there is no turning back.

The parking lot at the Newberg-Dundee Police Department is an endless row of cop cars. I don't even have the courage to unbuckle my seat belt, so Alan does it for me, and he takes my bag.

"Come on. The sooner we do this, the sooner it's done," he says, rational, poised, supportive. But there is nothing rational about telling a roomful of officers that I was raped by a group of jocks. There's nothing rational about reporting a crime that took place over a year ago. And there's certainly nothing rational about willfully slicing open the place where I carefully store my misery, essentially inviting the pus of that festering infection in the depths of my heart to now come oozing out.

"I can't do it," I say, clutching the armrest in the car. We're here because Alan has convinced me that I absolutely must make an official statement about what happened to me, if only to stay within the statute of limitations, so that I can press charges one day, *if and when* I am ever ready. I trust him, his mind and his maturity, so I agree, knowing, of course, that it will feel like open-heart surgery.

"You're stronger than you think," Alan says, and for a second I believe him; and in that split second, I manage to get myself out of the car.

From the moment I walk into the precinct, my senses feel heightened. The sound of my soles against the floor feel loud and unnecessarily percussive, and even the shuffling of paperwork sounds like a loud serpentine hiss in my ear. The cops all have poker face stares, each one busy and seemingly unconcerned with us. Walking down a long corridor to the room where I'm meant to report my case, I start to wonder if experiences like mine are often reported here, if these types of stories are old hat for these stern-faced, uniformed cops, who seem impervious to everything. I haven't even thought of what I will say, how I will start, which words I will use. Will they blame me for sneaking out, for hanging out alone with a bunch of drunk and stoned guys? Will they think I had it coming?

Alan holds my hand the entire time; this has become his signature, a constancy that shows me he has my back, that's he's not one of those boys, that the possibility of something good is out there.

I'm seated in an empty room. One of the officers brings in the sweetest golden retriever I have ever seen, an emotional-support dog, for me to cuddle while I talk. The overgrown puppy stays right by me and looks straight at me, her own giant brown eyeballs practically saying *I love you* the entire time. And in that room, with one hand in Alan's and the other caressing the top of that sweet puppy's velveteen head, I tell my story, one agony at a time, everything from the early bullying, to the daily violations at school, to the piercing solitude, to the daily crying in the bathroom, to the night of the rape. *I use the word "rape,"* shocking myself with every flash of memory, vividly reliving the hell one hideous snapshot at a time. A part of me is detached from what's happening, as if watching from above, unable to come to grips with this insane narrative that's spilling out of me, as if it wasn't me who experienced it. But I begin to sob so much, so intensely, the words thundering out of me so emphatically, my body shaking so hard, that I know it's me, and the cops tell me to take a break, give me a glass of water, and let me wear my sunglasses for the rest of the session. I am asked to give a list of names and identify the boys in photographs, and each time I say one of their names out loud or see one of their villainous mugs, it feels like someone has taken a machete to my heart, until I utter the last name, Ivan's, and weep with a fierceness, with every one of my organs, my whole body crying out for what he did, for what they did, for how they changed me, abused me, took me from myself.

I've cried so much that my eyes are puffy to the point of unrecognition, but my angel Alan tells me that I have never looked more beautiful. My whole body is still quivering, and my mind staggers somewhere between past and present. One of the cops explains the logistics of "what's next," which would involve a long, arduous, and complex process of going to trial, complicated even further by the fact that I no longer live in Oregon. They explain that I can press charges whenever I want, and they agree to keep my notes and statement for whenever I feel ready. They tell me they are proud of me for being so brave. A female officer stands up and comes around to where I am sitting, and puts her hands on my shoulders. She tells me it's going to be OK. "You'll see," she says, squeezing my shoulders with a motherly touch. "Now that you've spoken about it, you can start to let it go."

WALKING with a friend
in the dark is better
than walking alone
IN THE LIGHT.

—Helen Keller

ANGELS & WARRIORS

The act of giving my statement to the police feels like ripping fresh stitches from my chest after surgery, my whole body cracked open for a public viewing, the skeleton of my soul exposed. I should feel better, but the opposite is true. Knowing that the truth is out in the world, somewhere filed away in a drawer, terrifies me, and there's this unshakable feeling that it's up for grabs somehow, that people can really know it, hold on to it, remember it, and, worst of all, identify me with it. But there is no turning back, and it's out there, officially a part of police records, which means I can never again pretend it didn't happen. Alan says that telling the police should make me feel better, but I can't help it, the opposite is true. What I tried for so many years to bury is now at the forefront of all my thoughts.

I start to realize that the notion of going to school—anywhere, not just in Newberg—still massively fucks with my head. Maybe it's just not for me. I have exactly zero school spirit, I ditch classes all the time and still manage to get decent grades, and when I am in school, it just feels like a giant waste of time. I have lost all interest in academia and idle on with mostly gloom. My mom hears about Truckee Meadows Community College (TMCC), which offers an education program in Reno in which high school students can attend college early. She says all I need is a high GPA and recommendations from teachers. "Those are no-brainers for you," Mom assures me. If I get in, it will be my third high school in three years, but at this point I don't even care.

High school teens get the chance to experience university life—and even the professors themselves don't know which of their students are high schoolers. It might be weird but I can see that Mom really wants me to give this a go.

She asks me to come downstairs to check the mail with her one day. We're both quiet on the walk to the mailbox. I know she's concerned because it's all over her face every time she looks at me lately. But when she grabs the stack of mail, suddenly I notice her face light up. She pulls out a letter and looks at the return address and holds it up to the light.

"What is it?" I ask, eager now.

She tears it open and starts reading out loud. "Holy shit!" she screams. "You got in, baby!" She can't contain herself and starts to cry, her whole body shaking, tears streaming down her cheeks, raining little saline circles right onto the acceptance letter. She grabs me close, the paper crumpling in her grip. I can feel her heart racing. I can feel how much she loves me. I fall into her, and we cling to one another in tears and quietly celebrate the prospect of new possibilities for me, and maybe for the first time we feel a tiny bit hopeful.

One day I'm settling in to my desk in a college debate class, when I see this tall, quirky-looking girl walk in. She's wearing rubber cowboy boots with skulls and roses on them, and has a look like she doesn't give a fuck. She's at once eccentric and brazen. I'm not sure why, but I have a strong compulsion to be her friend.

"What's with the boots?" I ask her, half smiling.

"What's with the questions?" she jokes back. And both of us laugh, for that split second feeling a unique connection. I haven't had a girlfriend since middle school, but Alexa feels like home. And even though I have misgivings now about female friends and their cattiness toward each other, with Alexa it's never like that. Alexa is simply the best.

She listens without judgment and she's all in when I need any kind of support, be it emotional or logistical. Her family takes me in as well, and they even give me a job working with plants at their nursery and doing some basic customer service. They open their home to me and always make me feel welcome. I don't even have to call in advance. Alexa's mom runs a tight ship, and their house is always spotless, with everything exactly in its place. Her mom even feels comfortable enough with me that they tell me where the secret spare key lives! I love that and bake for them as a thank-you for being so great to me. The whole family feels like relatives from day one, and right away the presence of this new cast of characters in my life feels like a move in the right direction.

Alexa and I carpool to school together and sometimes grab breakfast at Denny's or IHOP after first period. During some of these quiet drives, we listen to music and I think about our closeness and how lucky I am to finally have someone like her in my life. A friend. A real friend. Not just someone who will hang out with me, but someone who loves me and whom I love back, who makes me laugh, who gives me time, who shares her life. The more time we spend together, the more inclined I feel to really talk to her, to tell her everything.

"I'm pretty sure I was sexually assaulted when I was fourteen," I say one day, almost too matter-of-factly and taking an overtly noisy slurp of my Frosty immediately afterward, to obscure the weight of my own words. Alexa pulls off the road sharply and stops the car. She doesn't say anything, but her eyes tell me to go on. "It happened on Halloween," I say. And I proceed to let her have the whole thing; every shred of every detail that I can summon comes tumbling out of me now, and my new friend receives it, absorbing some of the hurt for me so that I don't have to bear it all—if only for that brief moment. She holds me, she lets me cry. She cries, too. And then, as if on cue, as if our worlds were meant to collide at this precise time, she says, "It happened to me, too." And in that moment, Alexa and I fall into a deep understanding of what it means to be a woman, and we lock into a sacred sisterhood. She listens without judgment, her eyes glossy and serious. This is what friendship is supposed to feel like, I think to myself, as if tasting the most basic of fruits for the first time.

Things at school feel a lot better. This new program works out perfectly because we receive both high school and college credits for all our classes, so even though I'm technically in community college, I'm also getting all the credits required to earn my high school diploma. Switching schools means I'm busier, more active, and have less time to wallow. Sadly, it also means that I see less and less of Alan. I have way more schoolwork, and it's a lot harder; I have Alexa in my life now, and there's just not a lot of extra time. I feel like I have stuff to figure out, and maybe what I need right now is just some me time.

There's an expression: "Some people come into your life for a reason, a season, or a lifetime." Alan came into mine for some very special reasons. He saw me for the person I am. He nurtured the best parts of me. He opened his heart. He believed in me. He rooted for me. He went out of his way for me. He dug me out of my own grave and brought me back to life. He was the angel who helped me confront my demons, and for this I'll always love him. But I have to let him go. Life feels too complicated and textured and messy for me right now—there's no reason to drag him down, too.

"Maybe you should take Paige to Ken Shamrock's place," Mom says to Dad one day, the words "Ken Shamrock" spoken in a way that suggests I should know who he is. She's sick of seeing me mope around all the time, and I know she also wants my father and me to spend a little more time together. He's been so busy with work since we moved to Reno, but Mom knows he and I have a bond and that we're good for one another. Lately, she'll try anything to get us to hang out. I'm tired and not particularly in the mood to go to any gym, but I pull myself together and head out with my pop.

Dad says Ken Shamrock, the owner of the gym, is a world-class legend. *Cool*, I think, not particularly impressed, but mostly because I feel indifferent to just about everything. When we arrive at the gym, it's Ken himself who greets us. The guy has small, deep-set eyes and a wide nose that looks like it's been broken at least fifty times. He's all shoulders and pecs, and his muscles are so fibrous and dense that he has the carriage and demeanor of a bull. He cracks jokes and unleashes a smile that says, "I'm smiling like this because if I want to, I can kill you." But despite all that grit, a certain warmth emanates from him, and right away I feel at home in his care. Dad says Ken Shamrock is a UFC Hall of Famer, a retired pro wrestler, one of the greatest MMA fighters of all time, and often referred to as "the most dangerous man in the world."

"Welcome to the Lion's Den," Ken says to me, his handshake so firm I can feel it all the way up to my jaw. Looking around, I feel both intrigued and intimidated. The place isn't a regular gym—it's a grungy, dirty, musky dungeon with a stench so potent I almost gag when we first walk in. It's as if a man's dirty reeking armpit has literally just hit me in the face. But rankness aside, something about this place is strangely comforting to me.

There's a sparring ring, a fighting cage, cardio machines, weights, and tons of beaten-up black punching bags hanging from the rafters, swaying in the space like hunks of drying beef in a meat locker. There's not a lot of talking, but there's plenty of grunting and heavy breathing, the sounds of kicks and hits, the sounds of air being chopped by the swoosh of a sharp strike. A giant and menacingly realistic lion made of brass sits proudly on the mantel of Ken's office, flanked by photo collages of famous fights and fighters—a history of victory, a time line of glory. But what I notice most is that this is a girl-free zone. Not a female in sight, save for Ken Shamrock's wife, who works in the gym. No girls means I can just be me. I don't have to chat. I can relax into my athleticism. The tomboy in me perks up.

The fighters are all focused in their own realms, whether it's weights, boxing, karate, wrestling, sprints, or deep core work on a mat. There are battle ropes and gargantuan kettlebells and giant tires and racks and racks of rusty-looking weights. There are shelves lined with pads and gloves of various styles and sizes, all of them worn out and stunk up to high hell. There are young scar-less fighters with smooth baby faces and pitbull-puppy fervor, and there are more seasoned fighters with jagged faces like Picasso paintings. Their busted limbs taped up and wrapped in crazy patterns on their bodies. The real common denominator here is that absolutely everybody is working his ass off. Whatever the task, the room as a whole feels like a constellation of individual missions, every man focused on his next big goal. This isn't a regular gym— this is a place to grind out progress. It's exciting to be here with Dad, too, a small peak into the world I know he loves. Being by his side here almost feels like a rite of passage.

Ken teaches us how to do heel hooks, which is when you wrap your opponent's leg with both of yours, and hold his foot in his armpit. Ken explains that you basically have to use your legs to control all his movements while his foot is twisted by holding his heel and forearm, and then you use his whole body to generate a twisting motion, which properly busts up his ankle. This, I think, is cool. From the start, my body knows what to do. As he explains, I start to understand anatomy as a kind of puzzle.

Ken looks on with focused eyes as I practice my heel hook on my dad. Having Dad as a training partner feels good, and for the first time in a long time, he and I are back where we've always been, father and daughter locked in the thrill of a fight. I zero in on the strength of my own grip, moving my body with the force of certainty. I listen to Ken's words as he walks me through the move, led by my intent and my curiosity. I've got my dad good. And for the first time in what feels like a decade, I swear I catch my father smile.

I KNOW who I am, and
that NEVER changes.

—Urijah Faber

THE HOTTEST LOVE

has the coldest end.

—Socrates

DRUNK ON CHAOS

I still feel a dull pain in my heart. It's one that I've grown accustomed to living with, like a recurring migraine—it's just always kind of there. But spending time training at Ken's gym and Alexa's friendship are the only things that feel somewhat good. The seriousness of the gym lures me into a tranquil, focused zone. Ken runs a tight ship, with a zero-tolerance policy for cussing or pouting. There's an air of unapologetic discipline in the gym, which helps keep me steady. I'm mostly boxing for now, but when Ken says I'm ready, I'll get to start grappling and trying some other basic martial arts moves. Even on the days when I feel most down, I go there and try to draw up some energy.

But while the tomboy side of me thrives at the Lion's Den, the sixteen-year-old teenage girl is eager to play, which is perfect, because that's when the mysterious and sexy Seth walks into my life.

"'Sup," a sly-looking guy says to me one day after school, lean-ing on his BMW, looking as casual as can be. There is intrigue laced into his gaze. There's something simultaneously handsome and punk scruffy about him. I recognize him, but I can't tell how. "We were in high school together," he says, as if reading my mind. He's got a tinge of an accent, but hard to guess from where. He's not very tall, but he is sinewy and strong in his compactness. His muscles are fibrous and taut like dolphin flesh. There's a confi-dence in his gait, and he's not afraid to hold eye contact. He doesn't smile at all. I pick up on something broken about him, a sadness maybe. But instead of running the other way, I want to know more.

"I'm Paige," I say, offering a hand.

"Hell of a handshake," he says, with my hand still held in his. His skin feels good, the perfect combination of cool and warm. I don't want to let go.

Oddly enough, he's nothing like Alan. Seth is one of those hotheaded, rough-hewn, rebellious types, and for reasons I don't really grasp, I'm totally drawn to him. I like his fire, his fuck-you-ness, his way of walking around like he could literally give a shit about all of it. As if the rules don't apply to him.

He comes over to our place and plays pool with my parents, carrying himself like a king. He has a lot of free time, which he says is because of some lawsuit—he's waiting on a possible million-dollar settlement. He doesn't go to school or work, and wants to spend every waking minute with me. There's something about his passion and full-throttle approach to life that turns me on. It's beyond feeling wanted—for the first time in a long time, I actually feel alive.

For the first six months, he clings to me, stuck to me like a piece of Velcro wherever I go. The texts start at seven a.m. and go on until I'm getting into bed. If I don't text right back, he calls. If I don't pick up, he calls again until I do. This goes on until he has my undivided attention. One would think that might get annoying, but there's a protective quality about him, a persistence, that makes me feel loved and unconditionally safe.

"Where were you between the hours of four and six p.m. on Tuesday?" he asks me one night. I have to look in my phone calendar to remember.

"I don't know, the gym probably?" I reply, not realizing that for Seth these types of details are important.

"I was trying to call you. What if something had happened to you and I couldn't get in touch? You gotta be smarter than that, Paige," he says, always with an air of *I'm here to protect you even against yourself*. Instead of feeling squelched, I allow his intensity, I am maybe even flattered by it. It makes me want him more.

He also doesn't approve of me taking the bus alone, or even walking, insisting that he drive me wherever I need to go. He behaves as if someone has appointed him to the role of my lover, chauffeur, and bodyguard, and anything I do to challenge this trifecta of duties is often met with extreme anger and heavy bouts of tension between us. He blows up and I calm him down, the two of us caught in this up-and-down landscape of lusty emotions. It's exhausting, but it's also sexy and passionate.

He even complains whenever I'm with Alexa.

"What about *me*?" he meows when I announce that I am going to her place, which I often do. Why wouldn't I? I love Alexa and her family—they happen to be one of the main reasons why I feel settled in Reno. "What does Alexa give you that I don't?" he asks rhetorically with a fiendish smirk, stretching the word "Alexa" out like it's a joke in his mouth. But each time I make a plan with her he seems even angrier, and at one point he literally blocks the doorway of his house so that I won't leave. At first, I think he's joking. *Who would really do that?* But he presses his weight hard against me when I try to make it out. Seth, I learn quickly, is not here to fuck around.

Alexa doesn't like his vibe one bit, but she's happy for me so she mostly stays out of it. We learn to navigate that sacred space between girlfriends where there's a certain amount of respect given to the "guy" in one another's lives. Even though he makes her mad, she gives me the room to figure it out.

Another time I tell him that my mom and I are going to a concert.

"How nice for you guys. Did you get me a ticket?" he hisses.

"No . . . my mom got them. Come on, don't get mad," I coo, always trying to keep it playful with him. Things can turn quickly with Seth, so I learn to keep my tone light.

"Your mom doesn't want you to be happy," he says, the words dripping with resentment. "She's obviously neurotic."

"Why would you say that, Seth?" He's adorable, but he can be a real dick when he wants to.

"Because she wants you for herself when you should be spending your time with your boyfriend. You're a teenager, not a toddler!" he screams, trying to educate me. "What mom takes her daughter away from her boyfriend on a Saturday night?" This is how he tries to convince me that my mother is too overprotective and that I owe it to myself to cut the cord.

"You can come with us next time," I say, knowing full well that my mom can't stand the sight of him, so there likely won't be a next time—at least not with her. He gets really riled up and punches the floor so hard that he breaks his hand, splinters of wood sticking out the flesh of his palm like bloody thorns. He rolls onto his back right away and starts crying like a little boy who has just suffered an accident on the playground. I cradle his head and tell him it's OK. I don't know why, but I feel the need to take care of this person. His drama matches my latent sadness in a way I can't explain, but that somehow makes sense to me.

Another time we're hanging out at his house, just kicking around watching a movie. We're all cuddled up on his sofa, and things are calm. Until my phone rings. It's my mom, so I get up to go into the other room to take the call—not for any reason in particular other than the TV is on too loud and I simply want to be able to hear her better.

"Hey!" Seth yells, pausing the film. "Where ya going?" He cranks his neck to try to scope out my phone, to see who it is.

"Just to the other room," I answer, with an expression on my face that says "Why does it even matter?" "It's my mom," I say, emphasis on the *mom*.

"Why can't you talk here?" His eyes are narrowed now and his chin is tilted up. This is the moment when I know he could flip. I have to stay level.

"Because I can't *hear* anything," I reply, now a little irritated.

"You got something to hide?" he says, standing, his tone sour and his brow tight.

"Really? It's my mom, man. Calm down."

"Don't tell *me* to calm down!" And he hurls his plate of pizza across the room, sauce everywhere, porcelain shattered.

"Jesus, Seth!" This type of antic reminds me of my dad's short fuse. So I stare at the slice of pizza that's sliding down the wall in slow motion and then, in an act of pure deflection, I start to laugh, and so does he, and that's the end of that . . . at least for now.

My mom doesn't feel at ease around him at all. She says he's got a darkness. I tell her to relax. Dad doesn't care what I do, as long as I'm not sulking around the house all the time. He also doesn't mind Seth's no-bullshit character—it reminds him of himself.

"Don't you want me to be happy?" I ask Mom rhetorically, laying the guilt on thick. And I mean it. After the shit I've been through, I would think she'd be happy that I have someone new in my life who I actually like. Seth might be right: Maybe I do need to set boundaries with my mom. Maybe part of my problem is that I'm not independent enough. So I sneak around, I disappear and come and go like a shadow, I hang out with Seth whenever I want, and I don't ask for permission and don't give explanations. It's my life and I'm driving.

On Thanksgiving weekend Seth comes with us to Newberg to visit with family. Thank God he is with me, because just being in this town, especially in the fall, makes me want to tear my hair out. Being here feels like visiting the graveyard of someone you never really liked, like I'm meant to somehow pay a certain respect, but no part of me wants to be there. The fact that so much of my family is here is the only thing that makes the experience bearable, and with Seth by my side, I guess I should be OK.

The afternoon before the big dinner, he and I are at the grocery store to pick up some stuff for my aunt Cara, which I'm somewhat excited about because I've been experimenting with cooking lately, and I'm eager to help Cara out with the meal. I'm standing in the condiment aisle looking for ground nutmeg, when out of the corner of my eye I see a huddle of people at the other end, snickering and gesturing toward Seth and me. I can't tell what exactly is happening, but something about the menace in their stance and the way they are directed toward me makes my skin go warm.

"Tell that slut to get the fuck out of our town!" one of them yells through cupped hands on her mouth, half wanting to be heard and half hiding. Seth doesn't know anything about my history here, so the last thing he thinks is that they could be referring to me. He doesn't do anything for the first few moments, and instead waits to see what's going to come out of them next. It almost seems like he wants them to do something else. I try to turn around and face another direction, to dodge any eye contact, to remove myself from the whole dynamic. They watch me fumble, cackling like a coven at the other ends of the aisle, reeling in their discovery of my presence. I knock over a whole row of spices, which rattle and topple like little bowling pins all over the floor. I kneel to pick some of them up when suddenly I feel something cold, moist, and fleshy smack me on the shoulder. They actually threw a piece of raw chicken at me! I totally freeze, unable to scream or even cry. Seth's face goes purple and the veins in his neck bulge into thick, pumping ropes. Both of his hands are in tights fists and his knuckles a yellow-white as he runs down the aisle, chasing the girls out of the store and into the street. I get up, wipe the stinking chicken slime off my shoulder, and follow them outside, where I see the girls jump like fugitives into their car.

"Come on! Get in!" Seth snarls, but it isn't even Seth anymore— it's an animal that's taken control. His eyes are wild, every one of his exhales exaggeratedly loud and sharp. I get in the car and before I even have a chance to buckle up, Seth is driving at top speed, chasing the girls in their mint green VW down the road.

"Stupid fucking cunts!" he screams, spitting the words through his teeth. He grits his jaw and screams hard questions at me: "Do you even know those bitches?" The look on his face says he wants blood. I sit shaking but silent, straddling the feelings of fear and vengeance. Part of me wants him to calm down, the other part wants him to smash their fucking faces in. They deserve to be hurt. They deserve to be tortured. We're going so fast that I grip the side paneling of the car with both hands.

"Jesus Christ, Seth!" I scream, because I can't imagine how this whole scene is going to end. He's closing in on the girls' car, and we get close enough for me to make out at least one of them: it's clearly one of the burly bitches who used to corner me into the lockers, who used to breathe into my face and steal money straight out of my wallet and scribble "Paige Slutton" all over my stuff. And the memories come gushing back, and now I'm not only screaming, but also crying hysterically, and the faster Seth drives, the closer I feel to justice.

The engine howls as he speeds up, then he rear-ends the back of their car, hard enough that it spins sharply to the right, careens off the road, and comes to a screeching stop, with dust every-where, and their shrill screams audible to me even though their windows are all rolled up. Seth bolts out and runs over to their car. Panicking, they lock it from inside, which doesn't stop him from taking the most violent swing I've ever witnessed from a living human, punching the side of their car so hard he leaves way more than a dent. The girls are now hysterically crying, calling for help. I sit frozen, watching the unfolding scene with a strange sense of redemption slowly filling me up. I feel a jolt of euphoria watching them squirm.

We don't talk about it on the drive back or ever again. Maybe he doesn't want to have to apologize for or explain his temper, and I certainly don't want to have to tell him about who those girls were and what it meant. It's like a sudden storm that comes and passes. But it moves me. Later at Thanksgiving dinner, I hold Seth's hand under the table, and silently give my thanks to Jesus. Seth stood up for me like a man. It was at once the most romantic and terrify-ing thing that has ever happened to me. *This must be love*, I think. He's clearly a maniac, but he's my maniac, and I'm safe with him.

BETWEEN LOVE & LUNACY

One Saturday night we're at his house cooking spaghetti, and as we always do, somehow or other we get into an argument about our plans for the next day. He wants the rundown. He wants to know how much I've made it a point to build him into my day. My schedule, it seems, is always going to be a raw nerve for Seth. I have to find a way to set some boundaries.

"I'm going to the gym tomorrow. I told you, remember?"

"The hell you are," he says, changing the channel, taking a long swig of his beer, and not even looking at me. "I told you: that fucking place is nothing but a sausage party." He hates that I'm the only girl there, and he doesn't get why I feel the need to train at such a filthy place. *Why can't you just go to a Spinning class like a normal girl?*

Sausage party or not, the Lion's Den is a refuge for me right now, and not even Seth gets to take that away from me. I like being there with my dad, and I like what I'm learning. While I'm there I unplug from the world. I release myself into the fullness of my physicality, demanding strength from myself at every session. It's where I blow off steam, where I reboot and where I push myself. Some girls like spin classes and yoga—I guess I like to fight. After what happened on Thanksgiving weekend, it's a good idea for me to learn some basic self-defense. I try to explain. I try to make him understand.

"Seth, don't be like that—you know going to the gym makes me feel good."

"*I* should make you feel good" he says, with a narrow-eyed glare. Everything threatens him. He never feels good enough. It's almost heartbreaking. I smile and go over to him, a gesture of good will and peace, in the hopes that he'll snap out of whatever mood he's in. But the next day when I get up and start getting myself ready to go, he leaves the bedroom—with me in it—locks the door, and says again, "I already told you—you're *not fucking going*! Don't test me, Paige!"

"We're *through* if you don't open this door!" I scream through the walls, banging the door with both fists. "I don't need this shit in my life."

"Ok, Paige. Dump me if you want. But then you'll be the one who has to live with the consequences when I *blow my mother- fucking brains out*!" he threatens. "Unless, of course, you're not alive either!" I can feel his mouth close to the door. I should be scared, but I'm not. I'm mostly just concerned about him. His dad abandoned him and his brother, and then his mom ditched them to go be with some boyfriend she met in an online chat room. So, he's no stranger to deep-seated issues and neither am I. I want to show him that I'll never abandon him, that I will always love him. I don't even care when he shreds my yearbook with his bare hands, after seeing that Alan, my ex, had signed it. I pick my battles. He can kick and scream and do whatever the hell he wants to the stupid yearbook as long as I can keep training.

I mostly try to keep Seth away from my folks. Alexa is the only one who knows the truth about his antics. At this point, she wants me to break up with him, but when I think about leaving him, the guilt hardens my heart and the thought of him suffering reignites my loyalty. I want to take care of him, to be the thing that stops his pain. I want us to heal together and come out the other side in love and happy. Maybe I need him as much as he needs me, so I drink up his chaos like a familiar elixir.

For my seventeenth birthday, my parents surprise me with an impromptu weekend to Disneyland, and since Alexa is also going to be out of town, Seth offers to watch my dog, Chester, at his place while we're gone. I haven't had much time alone with my folks lately, so it seems like the perfect opportunity to get away and bond. We're in line to buy a churro when my cell phone rings.

"Your stupid mutt crapped on my floor!" Seth screams from the other end of the line, without even saying hello, and hangs up.

Chester has never been a fan of going to Seth's house, so I wouldn't be surprised if he had a nervous accident. Fucking Seth, though. Can't you just handle it, dude?

After the weekend, I pick Chester up and bring him home, but there is something off about him. He's wheezing and snorting in a way that he never has before, and I can tell he's having a hard time just getting from point A to point B. He looks at me with his head cocked to one side, there's a strange froth on his black lips, and he whimpers whenever I try to pick him up. I take some comfort when I see that he's finally asleep and getting some rest, but when I get closer to caress him I don't see the familiar up-and-down motion of his belly. He's not breathing at all. Chester is dead! I start going crazy, screaming and crying and pacing around the house, and Dad rushes in to give him CPR. But nothing works.

Mom and I take his body to the vet, where they examine his corpse and estimate that he's likely suffered some kind of anaphylactic shock, maybe due to an allergic reaction to a fleabite. But it's just a guess, and I can't tell if it's just a load of crap.

"We can do an autopsy on the little guy, but that's gonna cost upwards of $1,000—so it's up to you," the vet says plainly, covering my beloved childhood pet with a thin white sheet, an act that feels so clinical and final to me. Mom holds me close and the two of us quietly sob for Chester.

Watching the veterinary nurses take Chester's body from the cold silver table off to God knows where, all I can think of is Seth. His rage. That crazy look in his eye. The sinister way he spits out the words "your mother," knowing that she wants me to have nothing to do with him. The way he flares his nose in irritation when I say I'm going to train or to Alexa's, or anywhere or to do anything. The way he squeezes me so tightly that sometimes it stops feeling like a hug. The way Chester used to scurry to the other side of the room when Seth would walk in. "Motherfucker," I mutter under my breath, seething. I know he had something to do with it—he definitely did *something*. Chester was perfectly fine before I left him in Seth's care. So irrational are the levels of that man's envy and possession that I wouldn't be surprised if he *was* actually jealous of my goddamned dog!

I don't even bother to do it in person. I send a decisive text.

don't call or write. i'm done with you.

I change my phone number right after I hit "Send" because I don't have the head to deal with what I know will be a barrage of texts and calls back from him, begging me to stay—or worse. I'm not afraid of losing him—hell, I don't even feel bad about abandoning him anymore. As far as I'm concerned, he deserves to rot in his own misery, and I want no part of it. I'm sick of his shit. The possessiveness. The onslaught of meanness. The meanness about my mom! My fucking dog. His fucking tantrums. The whole shit show. It's done. I'm out. I go to the gym that night and train hard. My feelings jumble up into a fire that explodes onto the bag. The coach tells me to settle down, that I'm going to hurt myself, but I ignore him and pound the shit out of my agony with both fists until my lungs are winded and my skin is raw.

*   *   *

Some months pass. Things have settled. I've moved on from Seth. I'm getting my groove back. It's Thursday and I'm riding on the back of a motorcycle with one of my new friends, Kenny, enjoying the simple normalcy of the moment, the easy sunshine, the crisp, dry breeze. It's been a while since I could just chill like this. Then out of nowhere, I see Seth's car coming up the hill, speeding. Right away I see the violence in his eyes, the fuming that seems to come from a wicked but elemental part of his soul. That lunatic is hunting me down. I scream. Kenny hits the gas, but Seth is close enough to hit the bike with a heavy force, and Kenny and I both fly off and crash onto the street. I can't tell if I have broken any bones, or where Kenny landed, or if he's OK. I try to stand up and see that Seth is already out of his car and pounding on Kenny, blood spurting from everywhere on Kenny's face.

"*Get the fuck off him, Seth! I'm calling the cops!*" I take my phone out of my backpack. But Seth, who for all I know is high on a bag of bath salts, won't be stopped. And if he strikes Kenny one more time I'm afraid the guy might die right there on the street. "Please, *stop*! Can we just talk!?"

Seth releases his grip on the front of Kenny's shirt and looks up at me, Kenny's head dropping to the asphalt with a thud, blood dripping from his nose and mouth.

"You're damn right we're gonna talk. Get in my fucking car, and we'll talk in private. And your shitbag friend doesn't get to come," Seth says, spitting on the street, perversely close to Kenny's mouth. I can't even tell if Kenny is conscious or not, but if I don't play ball with Seth right now, he might murder both of us, so I quickly get into his car. It is one of those moments that I instantly regret.

Seth locks the doors and tears off. He's breathing heavy and staring straight ahead. "Where are we going?" I ask, trying to keep calm. He doesn't answer, and instead accelerates even more. "Seth . . . please," I try again

"We're going somewhere where we can talk. Like grown-ass people. Without your mommy and daddy and bullshit new boyfriend to interrupt us," he says. What a bizarre déjà vu, to be here with him again, sitting in the passenger seat, while he drives like a mentally deranged criminal who just escaped from a ward. How did I find myself here again?

"OK," I say, acting like his plan sounds perfectly reasonable.

"You owe me two fucking things, Paige: an apology and an explanation," he demands, sure of himself and mad as hell. He's hurt because I dropped out of his life via text; I get it. I never called him back after Chester—I never even called to yell about Chester. I literally just deleted him from my life. I guess that's the kind of thing that could drive a guy like Seth insane. My strategy is to make him think I'm working with him, to not show resistance, which will only stoke his fire more.

"OK, Seth. We can talk," I offer up, wishing there was some way to telepathically call my mother or the police.

He drives for a while and far away enough that soon there are no strip malls or apartment complexes anywhere in sight. There's nothing but a vastness of tumbleweeds and far-off mountain silhouettes, and instead of traffic I start to hear the sounds of the high desert dusk settling into the night. Seth has driven us into the middle of fucking nowhere, and my PTSD kicks in with such fervor that I feel myself starting to hyperventilate. I don't know what this guy is capable of, but I know that he's insane, and if he brought me out to the middle of the desert, I am completely fucked. The best thing I can do right now is show him that I care about him. I can't show him I'm afraid, because he'll get defensive. I try to breathe deeply through the terror. He stops the car. There's nothing but dry earth as far as the eye can see.

"Get out," he demands, and I oblige, trying my best to remain composed, as if he's just brought me out to show me the stars.

"Let's just talk like adults," I plead softly, crossing my arms against the encroaching nighttime desert air. If I'm not careful, I can die.

"I'm gonna fucking kill you for what you did to me," he barks, his facial expression a blast of pure wrath. "*Why can't you love me?*" he screams into my face, a question whose answers he already knows. I did love him. I loved his passion, but it swallowed me up and turned me into a nervous mess. It pulled me from my best friend and family and it asked me to belong to just him, like a piece of property or something. It went from delicious to demeaning.

My legs are shaking, there are goosebumps all over my flesh, and the sand is starting to whip up into the wind. But I must think fast. So I do the only thing that feels remotely viable—I run like hell. I tear off so fast I can feel the wind sting my face and sand blows hard into my eyes, but I won't dare stop because he's chasing me with the same vitriol that he chased Kenny on the bike, and those girls during Thanksgiving—with the savagery of an apex predator hunting down dinner. I'm going as fast as I can, but now he's right behind me, because I can feel and hear the intensity of his breath. I turn up the speed, pumping my arms, sucking in more and more air so to keep myself going. I don't know where I think I'm going—there's nowhere to really go. We're in the middle of the desert.

And in the space of that self-doubt he catches me. He tackles me to the ground and turns me over so he's on top of me, face to face. With one decisive move, he rips my T-shirt right off my body, and then my bra. He's growling and moaning now, as if preparing himself for a death ritual. I'm so petrified I don't even feel cold anymore. And I can feel the presence of my demons now, lurking in the dusk, laughing at the irony of me being pinned down into submission by this animal who supposedly loves me, my clothes forced off me, my fear spilling over. I can feel their appreciation for this sick cosmic joke that's unfolding on this dusty desert floor.

"*I'm sorry!*" I scream at full volume. "*I love you!* Let's get back together!" It's all I can think to change the course of this mess. He moves his face close to mine, eyes to eyes and nose to nose, and I think he's going to kiss me, but he doesn't and instead squeezes me with the strength of a super snake and bites my lower lip so hard it bleeds. I start crying and now he does, too, and it's a swirling mess of blood, sand, and tears on both our faces, and I can't tell which one of us is more disturbed.

"I swear I'll drive us both off a cliff if you're lying, Paige!"

"I promise! I'll be with you," I say, sobbing now. He releases his full weight onto me, and cries hard into my chest, and I can hear a pack of coyotes howling in the distance. After a few moments, he starts to compose himself, gets up and pulls me up with him. We stand there together in silence for a moment, panting, both of us wondering what the hell went wrong, with this night, with our lives, with this love. Both of us experiencing our brokenness in the context of one another. He puts an arm around me, his fingertips digging hard into the fleshy part of my shoulder. He leads me back to his car and pushes me into the passenger seat, still breathing heavy. He can't help it—for him, love and danger just go together. He rummages in the back for a while until he produces a tank top, one of his, for me to put on.

He turns the car back on and starts to drive, and I'm quivering so hard I can hear my own teeth.

"Calm down!" he shouts. I stay quiet, trying to come up with a discreet way of texting my mom, but my phone is in my pants pocket and there's no way to get it without him seeing. I can't risk another one of his outbursts. I need things to just stay neutral until I can find a way to sneak to my phone. But he's driving in the direction of his apartment, and his headspace is so massively compromised right now that he's capable of anything at this point— especially behind closed doors. I fight back the tears and try to think. *How could I be such an idiot?*

At least we're back in the city now, and I'm so physically exhausted from the last few hours that against my better senses, I unwittingly start to doze off. The sound of a police siren startles me awake. The cop car is right behind us, and when I look around I see there's not one but four police cars hot on our trail.

"*Sons of motherfucking bitches!*" Seth yells, pounding his fists on the wheel like an overgrown toddler about to get the time-out of a lifetime. The cop closest to us demands through a megaphone that Seth pull over immediately, which Seth finally does, but then proceeds to lock us both inside the car. "Don't you fucking move. I'm gonna pretend I have a gun—I'll say I'm gonna blow both our brains out." His tone is even but his body shakes.

"Step out of the vehicle with your hands up!" the cop yells. Seth does nothing. He closes his eyes hard, as if willing the cops away with his thoughts. "I'm not gonna ask you again, son. Step. Out. Of. The. Vehicle," the cop repeats, each word now sharper and loud. One, two, three beats of silence—and then the main cop, along with the other three, are outside their cars, bulletproof vests visible, guns drawn, and they are inching their way toward Seth's car. Now we're surrounded by them—there's one on Seth's side, one on mine, and one in the front, facing us—all of their guns pointing straight at us. They clearly don't know I'm a hostage. "Roll your window down, *right now!*" says the cop on Seth's side. When Seth doesn't comply, the cop on my side instructs me to roll mine down. I look at Seth, in tears, and quickly do as told before he has a chance to object. Within seconds I feel the cold steel of the officer's gun barrel grazing the skin of my temple, and hysterically crying, I raise my hands slowly and meekly to show clear surrender. The policeman is close enough to see the fresh blood on my face, and with that he must understand that I am in trouble with the driver, and signals for me to move out of the car. He cuffs me and sits me in the back of his cruiser. The three other cops force Seth's door open, drag him out, and cuff him fast. He's arrested for battery with a deadly weapon, coercion, domestic battery, false imprisonment, and simple battery.

I learn that a passerby had seen Seth beating up on Kenny (who is OK but mad as hell) and discreetly took down Seth's license plate number. The cops have been looking for his car since. Seth ends up in jail for three nights, after which he somehow manages to bail himself out. I'll never know how he could afford it, or anything for that matter. That guy has the stealth and craftiness of an alley cat, and while it definitely concerns me, it doesn't surprise me that he gets out soon.

Two of the cops have me lead them back to the spot in the desert where Seth drove me, where we find my T-shirt and bra right where they were torn off.

"Ma'am, were you in any way sexually assaulted?" one of them asks sternly, his notepad flipped open, pen in hand. He puts on a rubber glove and puts my stuff in a plastic bag.

"No," I say, in reference to Seth—but in the recesses of my mind everything else is bubbling up and fizzing like hydrogen peroxide on an open wound. My ghosts are suddenly with me again. And I start to think that I must be cursed, that maybe God wants me to live as one with this pain for reasons that I can't comprehend. "He said he was going to drive us both off a cliff," I say weakly, and in that moment I half wish Seth actually had.

I'm with Alexa and finishing up paying for my burrito at Taco Bell. It's been a long school day, we have lots of work to do, and we just need to quickly fuel up. We grab our food, fill up our drinks, and start making our way out into the parking lot, when I see him come in. Seth—with his hands in his pockets and a demonic smile on his face. This is starting to get ridiculous. How does this asshole always seem to know where I am?

"Jesus, Paige!" Alexa says, glaring at me, clearly under the impression that I have something to do with his being here.

"Fuck," I say, and grab her arm. I haul ass, with Alexa in tow, and quickly find the side exit. We bolt to my car and speed off, but he's already on our tail in that crazy way that he does, relentless and deranged. It's impossible to comprehend what allows a person to think that this type of behavior is acceptable. What does he think I owe him?

He drives up to me, revving his engine even more when he gets close. Alexa screams. I keep driving, but I don't know where to go. I have to avoid ending up somewhere he can corner us. I already know his game. So I start driving in the direction of the police station, and by the time we're there he's nowhere in sight. Coward, I think to myself.

"Are you in any kind of communication with him?" the officer inquires when they question me.

"No way!" I respond. And I'm not. He's dead to me after what he did in the desert.

"So how do you think he knew you were at the Taco Bell?"

"I have no idea!"

The cop inspects my purse. Then he goes outside to my car, where he pokes around for about fifteen minutes and discovers that there's a tracking device on its underside. I can't believe it! He is a full-fledged sociopath. Alexa doesn't come out and say, "I told you so," but she always knew he was no good. She's a good friend, though, and sticks with me for the whole ride.

With clear evidence in hand that Seth has been following me everywhere, I'm able to get a restraining order against him easily. But I'm always looking over my shoulder to see if he's behind me.

Now when I train at Ken's gym it's not just to blow off steam. I'm not just there for a workout. I'm there to learn. I go several times during the week and watch some of the fighters practice hard-core moves like twisters, guillotine chokes, and flying knees, listening for the guttural sounds emitted from their opponents who fall like dead birds to the floor. Watching these guys, I start to think about the energetics of power, the primal dance of survival that happens when two humans are eye to eye like this, their adrenaline coursing like gasoline. Ken starts to let me spar with some of the rookie fighters, and right away I'm transported back to those grassy yards in Oregon, when I was the girl who hit like a boy, when I'd come home with someone's blood on my wrist and Dad would half smirk. The sparring now starts to feel like a moving meditation, or like a place that collects my disparate emotions and reassembles them all into a singular strength. Ken observes me quietly, arms crossed at his chest. "That's the way," he says after I hit someone good.

I'm ready to move on to some basic grappling moves, and Ken carefully matches me up with equal opponents. One evening I'm up against a new guy who has been training for a lot less time than me. He's short, if a little stocky, and his breath smells like dirt. *I can take him*, I think as the ref counts us off. Not even seven seconds pass and the guy has me pinned on the ground. Rationally, I know I'm not scared of him or this situation, but his weight on me and the feeling of his grip on my wrist and the drop of his sweat that lands on my face all send me into an unforeseen panic, my airway tightening and my vision blurring. I can feel my heart beating in every part of my body, and instead of fighting back I almost pass out.

Your breakdown is
a BREAKTHROUGH.

—Andrea Benito

WRESTLING WITH MYSELF

Alexa and I are at a party. A friend from school casually told us about it, and we figured why not. Get out a bit. Have some fun. There are all kinds of people there. A Lil Wayne track is playing loud on the sound system, the bass buzzing in the yard so loud I can feel it in my abdomen. Someone is making these special craft tequila cocktails that taste like juice and go down like water. With drinks in hand and the carefree abandon of a whole weekend ahead, Alexa and I bop our heads to the rhythm of the music, just happy to be out and letting ourselves unwind.

And then, like a recurring nightmare that creeps into even the soundest of sleeps, there is Seth. He pulls up in a fancy Range Rover, which is probably the only reason it takes me longer than a moment to realize it's him, and he parks it right next to my mom's silver Accord. He's here for me.

"No way," I say, dropping my drink, the cocktail splattering all over my shirt.

"What the fuck!" Alexa says, equally stunned.

He's walking over to us now, all pomp and swagger. Like it hasn't even crossed his mind that this is an actual problem.

"You need to get yourself a decent set of wheels now that you go to *big-girl parties*," he says menacingly to me from a distance. He may be a scumbag, but he's no dummy, and he knows a restraining order is not something to tamper with, especially if you're out on parole, which is pretty much the story of his life. "Your car looks like *my ass*," he says, chugging a beer. He drunkenly rambles on about his big settlement, which I imagine is the only way he's able to afford that new Range Rover of his.

"I'm out of here," I say faster than I can even think about it, and before Alexa has time to object or even offer to come with me, I'm in my car and speeding off. I can't believe he tracked me down again. It's been months! Is he seriously so purposeless that all he can do is concoct these insane schemes just to find me? Also, what good is a restraining order if someone's just going to violate it? How am I ever safe?

Then it hits me. Maybe *I'm* the asshole for letting someone like that into my life to begin with. I allowed it. I tolerated it. I *invited* this drama. I ignored red flags, I forgave things that weren't OK. I encouraged the passion. And the weight of this revelation pumps at my chest and stings in my eyes and I want to cry and scream and break something because somewhere in the reservoir of my truths, I start to intuit a thread of toxicity woven from my past into the now. And I begin to see myself as a vehicle of all this bedlam, deserving of Seth's mania and all the other shit I've received. I start to understand myself as innately damaged, as someone who was born into the world to suffer. I drive faster, unhinged, tears streaking my cheeks, the stench of tequila rising up from my clothes. I drive even faster, watching the city lights turn into blurry trails of color on either side of me, feeling the throb of my sadness like an all-over bruise.

Then the sound of a siren. And a neon red spiral of light flashing rhythmically. Behind me. *Fuck.*

All previous thoughts stop dead in their tracks, heap into a giant pile and collide with a wall of panic. I pull off to the right, the dread boiling in me. The back of my neck and palms profusely sweat and my heart goes from beating to pounding at such a speed that I have to clutch my chest and squeeze my eyes. In the rearview mirror, I see the footsteps of a policeman approaching my mother's car. He has a flashlight in one hand and notepad in the other. I may vomit. He's right at my window now. I roll it down; he must be able to see tears still fresh on my cheeks. The beam of his flashlight cuts like a laser into my field of vision.

"License and registration, please," he says, his body stiff but his eyeballs searching. My body turns into a mess of fumbling and fidgeting, fingers burrowing through my purse for my wallet, nervously digging around for the items, which I produce with a sweaty, quivering hand. "You OK, miss?" he asks, with equal parts suspicion and concern.

I am not OK.

"Yes, officer," I reply, the words barely coming out. He leans in closer, and there's nothing I can do to control the heaviness of my breath, very possibly bordering on an asthma attack.

"Have you been drinking, ma'am?" he asks, already knowing the answer.

Silence from me.

"Ma'am. I asked you if you've been drinking tonight."

I know I have to respond, but the shame and my parents' impending disappointment moves in like a storm confiscating my rationale. I turn my face upward to the cop. It's not an admission, but it's not a no either. "Ma'am, I'm gonna have to ask you to step out of the vehicle." And that's when I know it's over. That's when I understand that I have failed.

I flop the sobriety test, am cuffed and arrested. The letters "D.U.I." sear into my brain, thoughts of my busted future appear like hard-to-watch scenes emerging on photos in a darkroom. I sit in the back of the cop's car as radio transmissions come in and out, their static crackling in jarring blips. I stew in my own disbelief, unable to grasp the fact that I am currently among the transgressors, a person of interest, a fucked-up girl, a lost soul. No amount of weeping buys me any mercy from the officer. He calls my parents and solemnly breaks both of their hearts with the truth.

I cradle the weight of my head in my hands and try to never look up from my view of the dark gray scuffs on the floor, because even the tiniest glimpse of the jail cell will make the sobbing start again. It's three a.m., which means I have another four or so hours to go. I try to lay down on the thin mattress, but it smells like stale pee, and any amount of sleep I can achieve is laced with sharp pangs of sorrow and remorse. A slide show of heinous memories plays on a loop inside my brain, stuttering and stopping at the roughest parts, sometimes rewinding and fast-forwarding to even worse ones, micromoments of my existence like living flash cards moving so fast I want to vomit. One minute I see myself alone onstage, the hot spotlights burning my skin. I'm supposed to break out into a dance, but I have forgotten the whole choreography and there's no song playing. My limbs feel stuck, held into place, pinned into submission, suspended in front of a cackling audience. Then I'm alone in a corridor and the laughing audience has morphed into shadows that creep behind me and grow into monstrous shapes with each lurch toward me. Then I'm naked and those shadows have become distorted faces like masks that come up close to mine, laughing thick stinky smoke into my face. Then I'm in the throes of a cheerleading routine and I'm the flyer, but instead of being thrown up and caught, my body disappears into the cosmos and nobody notices. Then I'm on the alkaline earth of the High Sierra desert, a glob of Seth saliva hot on my face while the massive orange sun does nothing to stop it and drops into the horizon, pretending it saw nothing. I see myself whole, then I see myself broken. I see myself laughing, which quickly turns into a wail. I see a little girl on a BMX blazing down the road like a shooting star, but then her bike suddenly disappears and she goes tumbling toward oblivion until there is no trace of her, not even a hint of a memory of what she used to be.

But it's the look on my father's face the next morning that cuts through me the most. He sits slumped in the waiting area of the juvenile detention center, but when he sees me being escorted toward him by a policewoman, he leaps up from the chair and literally growls like a beast. Even the cop winces. He doesn't even have words. It's just a glare like a hatchet. After a session of paperwork being shuffled around, I'm handed back my purse. I can still smell the tequila on my shirt; by the look on Dad's face, he can, too. His scowl is so pronounced he almost looks disfigured, and even though he hasn't said a word, his thoughts blare at me.

We get out to the parking lot and my father lunges at me. I know he's not thinking rationally right now, and I don't blame him. He's fuming cuss words and threats, saying he's going to beat the sense into me if he has to, chases me around the lot like a hound, weaving through the rows of cars until I finally stop, winded, and throw myself into his arms, sobbing with such intensity that I lose my voice. Through raspy cries I try to tell him how and why it happened, that I left the party to keep myself safe, that I had no intention of getting into the car when I did, that I would never drink and drive, that it was all because of Seth.

But he doesn't say a word to me in the car on the way home—or for the three weeks that follow. He basically drives me home as if transporting a sick horse to a more quarantined stable. I am told—via email—that I'm not to leave my room for ten days straight. Mom brings me my meals and my phone is taken from me. After ten days, I'm informed that I'm grounded for six *additional* months, during which I am allowed out only for school and—to my surprise—to train at the gym. I guess my parents want me to have something productive in my life, something far removed from idiots like Seth. Mom stays out of it, mostly because Dad tells her to leave me alone. But I can tell she wants to talk to me, to hear things from me.

Using the force of my whole body, I pour all my anger out at the gym. I draw up the rage and release into the movements. I batter myself and the equipment around me. I have nowhere else to go. I have nowhere else to be. It almost feels like I have one job and one job only—be incensed. At the world. At myself. At Seth for being such a relentless psychopath. At my dad, for not understanding. And at my mom, for not standing up for me. Since I'm also not allowed to hang out with Alexa, I am alone with my fury. I am alone with the history of my pain. When I'm not in school I sit in my room and stew in all kinds of existential realizations. I trace my path. My choices. The consequences. I want to punch myself in the face.

At my hearing, I try to sit in the courtroom with as much dignity as I can muster. Mom has picked out a pair of sensible trousers and a button-down shirt for me to wear, and my hair is gathered up into a neat ponytail. On the drive over to the courthouse none of us speak. At the trial, she and Dad sit behind me— she is teary eyed, and he is grumbling. Thank God Alexa is there, too. I feel relieved when I see that the judge is a woman, and even more so when I see the compassion in her eyes. Instead of judgment, I feel her empathy, this sense that she knows I got wrongfully caught up in a mistake. She seems less intent on punishing me than helping me. The solemnity of the courtroom softens when she speaks, and suddenly I feel grateful to be in the hands of a caring, powerful woman. She can tell right away from my testimony that I am nowhere near an alcoholic. She also knows, thanks to other court files in which my name has come up, that Seth has given me significant trouble in the past. And in a moment of what can be described only as an intuitive understanding, the judge gives me my sentence: it's not even a DUI, but rather a "wet reckless," which means all I have to do is sixty hours of community service, ten counseling sessions, pay a fine, and suffer a temporary suspension of my license—that's it. Since I'm still a juvenile, if I serve my sentence in full, all charges will be dropped. I don't feel good about having fucked up so royally, but I suppose it's here at the bottom where I really start to learn.

Dr. Morgan's office feels less like an office and more like a lounge. It's a room that inspires trust. The couch—laden with shaggy white cushions—is soft and deep, the kind that seems more apt for cuddling or napping than for delving deep into the recesses of the psyche. There's a vase with a fake white orchid in full bloom on the little coffee table between us, and she's got vanilla-scented candles on her desk that look as though they've never been lit but nonetheless perfume the room with a cozy, feminine warmth. Several boxes of Kleenex are placed strategically throughout the room, along with a small waste bin that sits at the foot of the couch. Dr. Morgan is serious but kind eyed, simultaneously poised and relaxed. She crosses and uncrosses her legs each time she asks a new question, and writes her notes with a pencil that always looks impossibly sharp. She sits at her desk with an almost methodical assuredness, as if from that position, she is imbued with the power to help improve lives. I am comfortable here with her and even curious about her. Hundreds of books line the shelf behind her: books about the mind, about relationships, about intimacy. My eyes land on one whose title includes the word "trauma."

I feel too nervous and timid to start talking, but since I must be there—by law—I decide to at least give her, and myself, a chance.

"We're not here to talk about what happened," she starts.

"We're not?"

"No, Paige—we're here to talk about *you*." And with that I understand that she understands, and I slowly allow myself to melt into her wisdom and care. I tell her about the person who I was before ninth grade, crying nostalgically, as if that person was buried, but buried alive and still fighting somewhere inside me. I tell her about how some of what I thought would be the best things in my life turned out to be the worst, and about how it felt to be hated, ignored, and mistreated, about the shame of never being good enough. I know the next thing I should tell her is about what happened that Halloween.

But then I stop talking altogether, my tongue suddenly heavy and thick in my own mouth. I've told this story before. I have uttered these words previously. But I stay quiet in the presence of Dr. Morgan, someone who I know understands, probably more than anyone else in the world, the gravity of what happened to me on that night. I stare at her fake orchid in silence, the truth pounding inside me.

"Paige?" she says. "Is there something more you want to say?" Dr. M. places her pencil on the table and removes her glasses. But the pain is too much now, and it feels like I might drop dead if I say even one more word. "This is a safe space, Paige. You can say anything you need to say. Even if you think it's stupid or irrelevant or unnecessary." *It's none of those things*, I feel like yelling. *IT'S FUCKING EVERYTHING.* I want to scream into her face. I want to hurl the fucking orchid into the next room. I want to shred her notepad into tiny pieces. I want to tell her she doesn't know anything about me. But Dr. Morgan must know what she's doing. She gets up from her chair, comes over to the couch, and puts a hand on my arm. She waits for me. She doesn't push. "Here we are, woman to woman, you are supported, and I am your support." And with that I fall into her arms and release several years' worth of cries onto that couch, and she keeps handing me Kleenex and just allows it all to unfold.

Throughout the remainder of our sessions I gradually tell her the story of the rape. And as I talk, I start to see myself in the context of my own story: my weaknesses stand up one by one, like recovering addicts sharing for the first time at a meeting, declaring their errors. All the red flags I ignored now flash in bright neon, as does the realization of how I found comfort chasing chaos long after the rape. I tell her that even my parents still don't know, that this secret has always lived in our house with us, but that they don't have a clue. I admit to her that sometimes I google my old name just to see if Ivan's video comes up. I tell her that I loved Alan but was afraid to be touched; and I tell her about all the mania with Seth, whose touch both electrified and terrified me. I tell her that sometimes I had wished Seth would kill me.

I tell her every detail of every moment of every misery. Sometimes she stops to ask me a question—"How did that make you feel?" or "How does it feel to talk about that now?"

And as we move through each pain, one at a time, looking at everything together, each one starts to hurt less and less. As if just by the act of observing, acknowledging, and discussing them we somehow relieve them of their impact on me. At one point in the sessions the focus shifts. We start to talk less and less about the past and Dr. M. asks me to bring more of my awareness to the present.

"What do you love, Paige?"

"Excuse me?"

"What makes you happy?"

"Happy . . ." I say, chewing the word in my mind as if it were the first time I'd ever heard it. I stare blankly at the orchid for a few beats, impressed with its majestic bloom, its awkward, gaping beauty. "I'm happy when I'm strong."

Around this time, I come across these lyrics from a song called "Rise" by Danny Gokey:

> There's a brokenness inside of you
> There's a wound that still reminds you
> Of the fear, shame, and rejection
> You have seen it, you have seen it
> You know it's time to get up
> But your heart's paralyzed, you're so stuck
> You're past the point of trying again
> You're defeated, you're defeated
> But something inside you can't deny
> You hear the call of your creator
> I made you for more, unlocked the door
> I wanna restore your glory

So rise
Breaking the dark, piercing the night
You're made to shine
An army of hope
Bringing the world
A radiant light
A radiant light
You were made to rise, rise
Lift your head and look around you
See the dreams you lost, they have found you
And the heart that once was beating
Is coming back to life
Coming back to life

So I zero in on the sweet spot—the balance between my counseling sessions with Dr. M. and my training sessions at the gym. I may as well, seeing as my parents don't allow me to go anywhere else. Dr. M. encourages me to keep training, to put my pain into my practice. Just like the judge at my trial, Dr. M. knows I am not a rebel or a troublemaker. She sees me. She knows what happened. And she's the one who helps me draw a line from weak to woke. She says training will empower me, and having clear goals will lead my way. I trust her not only because she is smart and experienced, but also because what she says resonates intensely with me. I start training every day. It becomes my place of refuge. My body becomes leaner, stronger, more flexible. More able. I'm like a two-way radio, taking what I need from those sometimes-heavy but always therapeutic counseling sessions and releasing their gravitas onto the bag or onto an opponent. With Dr. M. I explore the times when I was beat down, and then I pound the life out of those ashen memories at the gym.

I inhale the power.

I exhale the bullshit.

One strike at a time.

One day at the gym I'm paired up to spar with a girl who has been training for about as long as I have. I've seen her around before. She's definitely bigger than me; she's agile and with the kind of musculature that makes her look like she was hand-chiseled by God. We face off, hands up at our faces, ready. She takes quick, hard jabs at me, but I duck fast enough every time to elude her strikes, my torso weaving in and out of her grasp. I surprise myself. I'm not thinking about what's going to happen next. I'm in a flow state. She starts to get winded, her breath goes heavy, her eyes start to squint. And for a moment not a single thing in the world exists outside of this mat, outside of my fists; and with a strength born from a past place, I pull my elbow back and unleash an uppercut so fierce, a spurt of blood comes gushing from the girl's now-broken nose. She falls to the mat and I stand there with my mouth open in shock, sweet victory coursing through every single one of my cells. I stare at my hands and a deep awe overtakes me. Something elemental suddenly becomes clear:

I will always fight back.

Sadly, Ken Shamrock's gym has to move overseas. I'm sad to see him go. The Lion's Den is like a second home. I'll miss him and his whole family. The gym is very much a family-oriented business—his wife and kids are always there. They've invited me fishing and camping and it feels like being with them has been just as healing as the training. The question is, where will I train?

When I walk into a local gym in Reno and start sparring, some of the coaches stop what they're doing and turn to watch me fight. Some of them whisper. I can't tell whether they're impressed or surprised—probably a little of both. I don't particularly connect with anyone there, which is fine. There is no perfect gym. I have to take what I can get. Without a true mentor like Ken, I have to fend for myself. I don't rely on anything other than my intuition and my dad's advice to be my guide. When I train, I answer to myself. I am my own coach. And with that role comes the great responsibility to push myself even harder than I think I can deliver.

Through my new gym I'm asked to participate in an amateur fight. This is interesting. I've never been in a fight before. This would be my first official fight, which right away triggers the competitor in me, that once brazen kid who has been locked out and shut down. I can feel her again and she's hungry. She's not looking merely to survive the fight—this girl wants to win. She wants to go guns blazing, full-throttle, all in. So I accept the challenge and walk onto the mat for my first real fight with a surge of everything that's been quieted in me now blasting energetically at full volume.

When I walk into the cage for the first time, I try to breathe calmly and focus on shaking out my arms and rotating my wrists—but I'm totally blown away by the first-time-ever-ness of the whole thing. What a crazy concept: this designated space to fuck one another up, this weird little area where bodies relate solely on the basis of mutual destruction. It's more than a cage: it's a creative platform for all-out physical and mental human interaction. I'm home! It's so clean and empty at first, the energy perfectly still, but the potential is surging from both corners.

I face my opponent. The ref instructs us to touch gloves. My opponent stares me down, the fight unofficially kicking off with our eyes. For a flash of a moment I think about what this means, to stand here in front of another human armed only with the desire to kick her ass. I think about the goal—survival at all costs—and my heart starts to gallop. The bell rings and the cage instantly transforms into a stage and a human chess board, where our bodies and brains go to war. The energy swirls into a magnificent chaos, a primal human tangle manifested now in us.

But within just forty-three seconds, I choke my opponent out and win by submission, triumph pulsing in me, the feeling of redemption thick in my blood. And it is during this singular moment, fresh with earned victory, that I start to understand who I really am. The adrenaline takes over, euphoria flooding me. I laugh. I cry. I jump up. I grab my own head like a monkey. I run around the cage, fueled solely on the joy and disbelief of my win—a turning point happening in real time. I can taste it. And then, without even thinking, I unfurl both wrists and boldly hold up both my middle fingers at the crowd. It's not the crowd that I'm flipping off but it's the haters, those people who've tried to push me down.

I'm up.

My light is back on.

My weakness is turning to power.

I'm starting to rise.

The coaches at my gym start paying even more attention to me now. I'm not just "the token chick" anymore—I'm one of the strongest fighters around. I hear my name sometimes, people are talking about me—and not in a bad way. I feel like the coaches are starting to see real potential in me. They know I'm a rookie, but they see something in me, a fire starting to burn.

"We got a call this morning from a UWF promoter," one of them says one afternoon. "They want to know if you'll take a pro fight," he says, matter-of-factly.

"A professional fight?" I ask. I'm excited and already can't wait to tell my dad. He will freak.

"You can't do it," the coach quips, resolute, as if he came to this earth knowing what is best for me.

I look at him dumbfounded. "What do you mean? Why *not*? How could I NOT do it?!"

There's a $2,000 prize, and my family could really use the money. This would allow me to afford my schoolbooks and a few other purchases, which has been a budgetary topic as of late. If there's an opportunity for me to help out my parents financially, there's no way in hell I'm going to pass it up. It's not like I haven't been training. I can do this.

"Listen to me." His eyes narrow, his brow raised. "You need more training and more experience. The girl you'd be up against has a lot more of both than you do."

Most of the fighters that will compete in that event have fought tons of amateur fights—I'd have only fought in one. But even though I understand his rationale, I can't fathom *not* doing it.

"Once you go pro—you don't get to come back," my coach warns, his eyes locked on mine.

"That's good then," I reply. "Because I have no intention of ever going back."

The fight is going to be on June 30 in Corpus Christi, Texas, against Jordan Gaza, a professional Mixed Martial Arts fighter. I train harder than ever, on most days dedicating five to six hours to the gym. I take my cardio to new levels—if I can't hear my own breathlessness, I know I'm not working hard enough. I haul heavier weights. I eat cleaner. I sleep more. I start sparring with a training partner, Katia. She keeps me on my toes and pushes me to my edge. I am getting stronger with every session. A few days before the fight I go into the cage. The coach instructs five other fighters to take turns sparring with me—they're told to fight at 100 percent. I'm not afraid of this barrage. I am ready. This is it: if I can work through these challenges, this crazy matrix of unpredictability, one opponent at a time, I'm ready.

"Come on, hit me as hard as you can!" I scream. Don't see my gender. See my power. They come at me, one by one. Each fighter has a signature. I try to identify and lock on to it early, to learn quickly what I'm up against. These guys are strong and way more experienced, but I keep up. I hold my own. I fight back and I fight back hard. I make a decision to throw my whole body, brain, and spirit into every single strike. I'm drunk on the certitude that *I can fight back*. That *I will always fight back*.

With every hit, I reclaim my power.

With every evasion, I protect myself.

* * *

I'm in Texas. I'm so excited to be here, I don't even know what to do with myself. I feel the need to do this on my own and have left my parents at home. I don't even have a coach with me (he stayed back in protest); it's just one other teammate with me, and I barely know her. Usually, fighters come with a whole team of people—their "corners." But I'm here pretty much solo.

The day before the fight I walk the streets of Corpus Christi looking for a fight outfit and a place to braid my hair, amped on adrenaline but also dehydrated from the grueling process of having to make weight at 115 pounds. I weigh in and am cleared to eat! I head straight to Hooters with my teammate and we gorge on chicken wings and fries dripping with ranch dressing. That night in the hotel room we go to sleep with full bellies and high hopes.

On fight day, I wake up smiling.

There's a mass of people in the audience, the hum of their roars like the sound of the ocean. This is wild. I can't believe I'm even here. It's at once surreal, thrilling, and a teeny bit scary. My stomach feels like I've been on a roller coaster. My opponent is a high-level martial arts belt holder and a native Texan, so I'm in enemy territory, a major handicap already. She's wearing a hot-pink tank top and has colorful neon threads woven into her long braids.

I've wrapped my left hand first because someone told me it was good luck, and I've made a mental note to always do it this way going forward. Moments before we start I say an athlete's prayer that Mom texted me last night:

Lord, please clear my head of all distractions
And my heart of burdens I may bear,

So I may perform my very best,
Knowing you'll always be there.
Please lift me up before the moment,
So through your eyes may I see,
And have a clearer understanding,
As the game unfolds before me.
With great courage I will meet this challenge,
As you would have me do,
But keep me humble and remind me,
That my strength comes from knowing you.
Then when all eyes are upon me,
At the end of this game,
I will turn their eyes to you, oh Lord,
And to the glory of your name.
Amen.

Even though I am nervous as hell, the singularity of the moment grabs me. *I'll have the chance to do this only once,* I say to myself. *To be a first-time professional fighter.* And the force of that awareness fuels my strength and turns me into an impassioned machine with one goal: I have to beat this girl.

Our bodies lock in battle, brute force shifting back and forth between us. The cold metal pattern of the black cage presses against my skin each time as she pins me to it. She fights hard. But I come back harder. Still, though, I can't get her to tap out. We remain in this loop for what feels like forever, fighting for the power, refusing to give up. I start to understand that fighting is as much mental as it is physical, that having the psychological strength to withstand pain is just as crucial as being able to knock someone out. That fighting is about strength, but it's also about endurance, and throughout the rounds I fully commit to my own stubbornness. At times, I use both of my legs to wrap around her lower body, so that even though she's on top of me, she's in a locked position and can barely move. When she has me pinned, I strike hard into her ribs. After a while, I can tell she's starting to tire. She's slowing down. She's not initiating as much anymore.

I call on all my fury. I get even angrier. I call up more strength. I put in more fire. I rally every scrap of rage that I've dragged around all these years, and with the force of both my marred history *and* my mounting potential I fight to the end.

And I win. Three rounds, three minutes each.

It takes me a moment to comprehend what's actually happened. *"Paige VanZant!"*

When I hear my name called out, it doesn't register right away. I'm in a daze, trying to gather my bearings. My body is pulsing with something new, as if I have tipped the scale of my soul somehow.

The ref is standing between us, holding our hands, mine to the sky.

And that is the moment I know that I've risen.

I will get MY RESPECT
or I will die.

—Ken Shamrock

BORN TO FIGHT

O n the drive back to Reno, I watch the gray of the highway grow longer behind me and I think about the win. I have just won my first-ever professional fight; the adrenaline is still buzzing and the word "professional" echoes loudly in me now. What if I could really do this? Against all the odds, I came out and won. Hell, maybe I took the fight just to prove the vehement warnings of my coach wrong, but I think there was more to it. My spirit is dizzy on victory, and my mind surges with possibility. *What if I'm destined to fight?* These flashes of inspiration start to help me connect the dots of my life. I start thinking about where I've come from, my family's move, the crawling and clawing to survive, and I am overcome with a hunger to fight more. I realize that I've won; I've kicked the shit out of what was expected of me. I can rebuild a whole identity, a whole career, based on the power of strength. A life dedicated to the mastery of fighting back.

My dad and I sit down and have an actual meeting. He's pumped. This is basically his dream come true, to really be back in the ring, so to speak. "You need to strike while the iron is hot," he says assuredly. "If you're serious about this, you have to start fast and go full force. This is the time in your life to really get after something." I know he knows what he's talking about, and I suddenly feel lucky and grateful to have someone like him in my corner.

I keep training, but with a new clarity: I need to up my game. If I want to be a really good freestyle fighter, I need to be smart, but fast enough to act on my strategy; I need to be versatile, but savvy and selective regarding which skill to call on; I need to have stamina, but know how to pace myself for the long game. My cardio needs to be at superhero level, my grip stubborn, my confidence unshakable, my attitude positive.

But the more I train, the more I feel limited in Reno, since there aren't any good pro gyms around. I have this itching feeling that I need to go where the action is. I know this for sure: if you want to be a lion, you train at the Lion's Den—but if you want to be a professional fighter, you have to go to Las Vegas, the fight capital of the world. I imagine Las Vegas as a kaleidoscopic extravaganza of everything, a motherland of extreme excess, a twenty-four-hour playground built on chasing thrills. Life in Vegas probably feels electric, like time unfolding in blasts instead of moments. Big personalities with even bigger dreams. Loud music and bass, a vibration of revelry and the perfect backdrop for all varieties of debauchery. And because Vegas is such a popular tourist destination, people are there from everywhere. The whole attitude on the

Vegas fight scene is different. There, fighters don't just train—they self-cultivate.

"I'm moving," I announce one night at dinner. Mom and Dad both look up, exchange a glance, and wait for me to speak again. "To Las Vegas," I add. Dad narrows his eyes to zoom in on me, to feel me out.

"How can we help, honey?" my mom asks. Just as I slip more and more into my desire to be a fighter, so do my parents. They have my back and are the most loving and supportive people in my corner, as they've always been. All the fear and concern they were harboring about me now starts to soften into a loving admiration. Into respect. They are totally with me. They agree to help with moving costs and even chip in for my rent in Las Vegas, which I know is a big ask. They are somewhat more stable than they were when we first got to Reno, but millionaires they are not. But they've always been action-oriented supporters, and my move to the fight capital of the world is possible only through their unflinching loyalty and generosity. My dad is so glad to finally have his little ass-kicker back.

Saying good-bye to Alexa is harder than we both imagined. She's been the truest friend I have had as an adult, and the thought of sacrificing that for Vegas feels daunting.

"Stop being such a baby," I joke to her when I see her eyes well up with tears, which of course causes mine to do the same. I'm not particularly ready to say good-bye to her, but I've got my eye on the prize now, and I know it's not going to happen without a fair share of struggle.

I haven't given enough thought to where exactly I will live in Vegas, but then it occurs to me that I have a very old friend, Colby, who lives there with her family. This was a girl who knew me at my best, who saw me grind out auditions at age ten like a boss, who knew me before all the nastiness and drama happened. Colby's presence in Las Vegas gives me a sense of comfort, an anchor of familiarity.

"Can I stay with you while I figure out where to live?" I ask her on the phone one day.

"You can stay as long as you need to," she says, and she means it, because it's with her and her family that I stay for three months when I first arrive in Vegas. From the moment I get there, they take me in as one of their own without batting an eyelash. They make sure I have everything I need and include me in all their family meals and church-goings; they even set up a bedroom for me. At one point, when my back goes out, Colby's mom, Gaylinn, springs into action to help. Their collective sweetness and compassion feels angelic, and I settle into Vegas easier knowing there are people on whom I can count.

Colby knows I'm strapped for cash. She also knows how badly I want to be a fighter. She and her family brainstorm ways for me to make some extra money, and they eventually convince their church to give me some work. The church isn't officially hiring, but the board agrees to give me a job as a lunch lady anyway. I work every aspect of the kitchen, from prepping and cooking to serving a bunch of older ladies and happy kids. Everyone is gracious and kind, so the work is always a pleasure. I enjoy the mechanics of the kitchen and lose myself in the creative space of meal making. I play with spices, herbs, smells, and flavors, welcome sensory stimulation and a quiet refuge from the intensity of the rest of my life. Even though we make only basic comfort foods like pizza and tater tots, I love working with my hands and nailing the flavor profiles.

Thanks to the generosity of Colby's family, I'm able to save every penny I make at the church and train my ass off. In the course of a few months, I try out four or five different local MMA gyms that Dad suggests, but I never really connect with anyone in particular at any of them. No one takes me seriously either. I'm brand-new; I'm a 1-0 pro out of Reno, Nevada, with two fights total in my career. People mostly just look over my head. Everyone is busy doing his own thing, and no one really seems to take any interest in me. Which is fine, because I know what I need to be working on—wrestling, boxing, jujitsu, Muay Thai—and I make sure to get them all covered. Each one has its own style and unique something. I love the immediacy of wrestling, how you're all up in someone's personal space with the sheer force and pressure driving. I love how boxing demands agility and coordination. I love grappling on the ground for jujitsu, and I love the lethal dance of striking and clinching that comes with Muay Thai. No matter where I am training, I always aim to have a morning practice, an afternoon practice, and an evening practice, each hour-long session focused on one of the different martial arts. Between that, a lot of cardio and weight training. I'm doing a lot.

I can't live with Colby's family forever, so I scrape together what I have saved from work and what my parents chip in for me to move into an apartment of my own. It'll require living with a roommate, but it feels like a healthy, independent step. One day at the gym I run into Catherine, someone I knew from Reno who apparently just moved to Vegas and is looking for a roommate. We've never been close, but we decide to move in together to make ends meet. At first, I'm excited about the prospect of living with a fellow fighter. I hope that we can bond and maybe she can share some wisdom with me or knowledge that I can learn from—but sadly, she turns out to be a terrible roommate. She has sleazy guys slinking around our tiny apartment all the time, and she's constantly late with rent. It's better than being alone, but just barely. "Catherine, if you're going to finish my milk every two days, can you at least sometimes buy a carton of it yourself?" is something I find myself regularly saying to her.

For my fighting career to evolve, I need more support outside the cage. I need someone to help me find and secure fights. I do a little bit of Internet research, which leads me to Max. He says he can help me pick up some fights, so I begin a casual correspondence. Not much comes of it, until I get the call about my second pro fight.

"We need a nickname for you," Max (whom at this point I have never met) says in an email. The whole nickname thing is just part of the theater that comes with MMA. It helps fighters develop personas, and it keeps things playful with the crowd.

I call up my dad; together we google fighter name ideas and come across "Twelve-Gauge Paige." As a country girl, I know it's the one.

* * *

If I win this one, my second pro fight, I'm officially on the path. My conditioning is more advanced than ever, and I'm feeling very strong. I go into the fight knowing how bad I need to win it. Colby's brother Bryce drives me to the airport super early to make sure I don't miss my flight to Fort Worth, Texas.

The event is called Premier Fight Series 2, and this time I face off with Amber "The Apex Predator" Stautzenberger, who is making her own professional MMA debut. She's taller and has longer limbs, so it's crucial that I tie her up fast and keep our bodies close. Otherwise, she'll try to use her length on me and hammer me with punches and kicks, assets from her jujitsu roots. She's a talented fighter, but there's something bubbling in me that squelches any sense of self-doubt.

At one point, she's on top and has me pinned good. I have to get creative and fast. Our feet are so close to the cage that I use mine to push off, which gives me just enough leverage to wiggle out from under her, a move that amazes the crowd. I snap into offense. When we're standing, we trade lots of close-range knees, but I do everything I can to close the distance quickly. I have to direct the fight to keep it where I want it. And no matter what happens, I don't submit. That's my bottom line.

We get right back into that stubborn embrace at the top of round 3 and I'm still driving. More than anything it's a wrestling match right now. I mount her and she throws me off, but I land into a guillotine. She throws punches to my ribs, but I don't even feel them. And with thirty seconds still left, I know I've won even before it's made official.

It's as if every win reignites a new part of me, and each fight gives me another notch of certainty: This is what I am meant for. This is who I am. It feels like every moment of my life has built on itself and maybe this was God's plan for me all along: to endure all the pain so that the triumph would taste that much sweeter; to struggle as a means to push further. The revelation hits like fireworks or a bolt of lightning. My pain is my path.

One day I get a message on social media from a name I have never before seen. I'm always wary of this kind of stuff, so I ignore it for the first few days. But then I get another one. It's from a fight promoter with Invicta Fighting Championships, the biggest all-women mixed martial arts league there is. They want me to sign a four-fight contract. I'm psyched. Fighting in a league of this caliber means I'm not out there in the world on my own. It means I officially am part of a posse; it means I'll have a trajectory. It means I'll have fights lined up regularly! Life suddenly starts to feel very real.

As part of this league, I face off with Tecia Torres, a killer Muay Thai fighter who's as fast as she is strong, and who is probably more technically advanced than me. The fight goes down on a blustery January day in Kansas City, and I'm out there with one other teammate and the one coach who managed to free up some time for me. Torres does everything she can to achieve my submission: she violently chokes me out, she attempts to dislocate my elbow, and she grinds me hard into the mat with the whole weight of her body. But every time she has me pinned, I scramble, manage to break out and stand up. We're in this cat-and-mouse game in which she definitely has the upper hand, but even so, I am making her work. I know I may not win—but I also know I'm not giving up. And the more we go at it, the clearer it becomes that the fight is hers. And yet every time I escape one of her choke holds or get back up after being thrashed hard onto the floor, the crowd goes wild in disbelief. The fact that I still believe I can do it emboldens the people.

But I lose.

I leave that cage defeated. Physically, emotionally, and spiritually. It's my first fight with Invicta—and I lost. And to make it worse, I am alone without anyone with whom to mourn it. I barely know the teammate who came with me, and I feel so embarrassed, I wouldn't want her consolation anyway. The loss feels like being pushed off a cliff and completely forgotten.

People say it happened because Tecia is more advanced in her career—that's what the Vegas coach said, anyway. But I don't care about the reason. The idea of all those people watching me lose is devastating. In the same way that winning is the most incredible feeling on the planet, losing breaks my heart. I fall apart, almost literally; I feel that everything I've worked for is broken. It's very public, and all I can think about is getting the hell out of there. I want to go back home immediately. I was wrong for coming in the first place. It feels like something precious has been suddenly snatched from my possession. When I call my dad, he doesn't mince words.

"You screwed up," he says, deadpan.

"I know I did. But how?" I don't care if he's mean—I'm here to grow.

"You went in with so much heart that you forgot your technique," he says, making me realize that *technique* really is the missing link for me right now. "Go in with your whole heart, but make sure that when you do, you're as skilled as you are passionate."

He's right. Moving forward, it's a precision game.

How do I get it back? How do I climb out? How do I recover? I don't claim to know everything about fighting at this stage, but I do know that I need every win. Each one propels me forward, building on the last one to sustain me. Losing, on the other hand, slows me down. It kicks my ass. And it humbles me.

But it also compels me to go harder. It demands that I dig even deeper. To push past my comfort zone and consider the possibility that this whole thing is going to be a lot harder than I thought. Just because I want to be a fighter doesn't mean I will. Just because I want to be a champion doesn't mean I am. *Until I am.* But it's going to take all of me. I'll have to make sacrifices. It's going to mean rethinking my whole approach. I head home replaying the fight in my mind, the whole time wondering what I could have done differently, and what I will do the next time.

When I pull up I see that no one is home. The apartment is empty. But it's not just empty in the sense that my roommate isn't home at the moment—rather, she's completely gone, and so are all her things. She's vacated the apartment. Not even a hanger is left in her closet. I never hear from her again, nor do I ever receive the last of her rent checks. She completely disappears without a trace, not a note, not a text, not a "have a nice life." All of this means I'm stuck with an expensive Las Vegas two-bedroom on the measly salary of a church lunch lady and the occasional few hundred bucks from the occasional fight. Oh, and the worst part is that she has apparently also taken off in *my* car (which I will later find out she has totaled!). I'm alone, I've just lost my first fight. I'm broke. And I'm out of a car.

Panic grips.

That April, I'm up against Courtney Himes in Grand Junction, Colorado. The good news is that the weight class for this fight is at 125 pounds—it's called the flyweight division, which means I won't have to cut weight drastically in a panic before the fight. I know Courtney is slightly bigger than me, but now that I can keep some pounds on, I feel stronger in my body. I say my prayer, take a deep breath, and commit to winning. From the moment we touch gloves, I'm driving the fight. The pain of my loss against Tecia is driving me. The need to correct the course of my career is driving me. I don't let up for a moment, grinding pressure into her the whole time, almost always from a position of dominance. She has me locked up on more than one occasion, but I slither out and slam her down, retaking the position of power each time. I win on a technical submission with a rear-naked choke. She glares at me when the ref raises my arm as they announce me as the winner.

I feel vindicated. Winning was key after that first loss, a public and private reminder of what I am here to do. But the win aside, financially, my stint in Las Vegas is starting to spin me out. It's frustrating to have all this drive and motivation but no real sense of direction. Scraping by on barely any money and not knowing when the next fight is going to come up. I feel like I lack real guidance and suddenly the Vegas period starts to suck more. Solo navigating all these new worlds: Las Vegas as a city, but also the fight world as a special club unto itself. I get the feeling that not everyone is excited about a new girl on the block. When I walk into the gym I can't make sense of the vibe: I get the occasional smile-less head nod—from both men and women—which tells me very little. No one is outright warm. People just seem focused on their own singular mission. Maybe overall it's been a journey for me to make friends, but in Las Vegas, it feels like I'm on a solo mission.

And more to the point, my folks simply can't afford to keep floating me extra money to make rent. They're struggling to get by themselves, and it's been so many years of them supporting all my different causes, it's time for me to start helping them out. The only logical move for me is to go back home. It's not ideal and it's not what I had in mind, but sometimes you just have to be tactical. There's something mournful about having to pack everything back into my mom's silver Accord, especially only one year after my arrival, but I try not to beat myself up. Careers don't happen overnight, I convince myself. I can pace myself. I can still train hard and fight professionally in Reno, where life is cheaper all around and I won't have to pay rent. Las Vegas isn't going anywhere.

I sit next to Mom at church, our shoulders touching. She holds her face up and listens intently, absorbing every word, using every moment there to connect. We've been going for the last few Sundays since my return home. I sit in the pew fanning myself, quietly listening, sinking into the calm of the collective solemnity. It feels good to press pause on everything and just be with my mother. Life's moving at a dizzying speed lately, so it's nice to have a moment when I don't have to struggle or plan. And listening to the pastor, the words suddenly reverberate in me.

> *Don't be afraid, for I am with you.*
> *Don't be discouraged, for I am your God.*
> *I will strengthen you and help you.*
> *I will hold you up with my victorious right hand.*
> —Isaiah 41:10

These precious words arrive at my consciousness like a warm, flickering light, lifting me up somehow. I take myself out of the sermon for a moment and think about how many times God has in fact saved me. I think of all those moments of panic that I have seen up close more than once, in several different capacities, when it wasn't entirely clear if I was going to live or die. I take a massive breath, breathing into the gratitude that wells up in me. Mom takes my hand. Something courses through us.

"I want to get baptized," I tell her after the service.

"Wow, honey. OK. Why now?" she asks, her eyes glossy.

"It's time to put God in my corner," I say, the truth of these words flowing through me.

"I'll do it with you," Mom says, always with me.

The sky above the Truckee River is an electric shade of blue, vast and bright, without a single cloud in the sky. We're standing by a cluster of large rocks, their smooth surfaces warm from the sun. I submerge backward into the water, allowing my whole body to fall into it freely, soaking into the story of my whole life, with the intention of coming back up stronger, more connected, more alive. I release more pieces of myself. I let go even more debris, the leftover damage that I thought had already passed but hadn't. I reflect on the totality of pain, thinking now about how the events of one night can become such an elemental story of one's life, how the rape not only damaged the most human part of me, but also how surviving its aftermath became my most crucial job. And as I thank myself for my strength, I go a step further: I make a promise to myself to recover the pieces of myself that were suppressed, ignored, or terrified throughout said survival, to reconnect with the strong girl I always was, the one who went after things, the one who would stop at nothing to achieve everything.

And in the new spaces, I invite gratitude. I surrender fear and welcome faith. I think about the importance of going into the ring with purity of heart, a heart connected to a force greater than myself. Now that I am a Christian, how much more could I give in the ring knowing that I am protected and supported? How much more could I accomplish by staying close to God at every level of the battle? If everything—in and outside the cage—I do and say is inspired by my belief in and love of God. A devotion to a force greater than me. So much of my life—good and bad—has centered on my physical body, and even my emotional body. Now it's time to nurture my spiritual body.

The baptism feels like a massive personal transformation, one that started when I changed my name and shed that first layer of identity that anchored me to the trauma. The next palpable phase of my change came with the revelation of wanting to be a pro fighter, when I tasted the glory of victory and what it could mean to live a life predicated on strength. The baptism now washes away all the memories of weakness and remnants of sadness, and in their place comes the presence of God. It somehow gives me a greater purpose for being a fighter. The ritual helps me become reborn as someone strong, focused, and faithful—a survivor who will forever take that faith and gratitude into any cage. I watch myself now, on this path of change, feeling in my bones and in my soul that with God in my corner, I can do anything.

I use my time in Reno to think critically about what to do next. I see it as an opportunity to regroup, to save some cash and get strategic. My parents are all in with me. They see how good this is for me. My dad is basically back in all his wrestling glory, and my mom is just glad to have me back and happy I'm involved with something that feels positive. They want this for me. We sit around the dining room table hashing out the possibilities, trying to figure out my next move.

"What's your goal?" Dad asks me, one eye narrowed.

I don't answer right away, letting the words rattle around inside me for a moment. I know, but I've never admitted it out loud.

"I want to be a champion."

He doesn't show it, but he's pleased with my answer.

"Well." He pauses. "To be a champion, you have to train with champions."

Around the gym, I start hearing about another Reno fighter who's doing well in Sacramento. Rumor has it that she's training with an MMA group called Team Alpha Male, an elite group that has earned the Top Fight Team title at both the 2013 and 2014 World MMA Awards. Dad says the team has some of the country's most seasoned experts in Brazilian jujitsu, wrestling, boxing, and Muay Thai, and that this place is a champion factory, regularly churning out award-winning fighters. He's especially intrigued because he says Team Alpha Male is known for having smaller weight classes in its program, which is perfect for me as a straw-weight, the division in which competitors weigh between 106 and 115 pounds. I toss around the idea of a visit to Northern California with him; and though we both agree it's a long shot to go out there, we decide it's at least worth a peek.

The drive through the Sierra Nevadas is as much charged with anticipation as it is with the unknown. I roll my window down and let the air hit my skin. I watch the greens and blues whiz by in a steady, infinite stream, excited about the plan but wondering if we're wasting our time. I'm in an interesting position: on the one hand, I'm a total rookie with only a couple of pro fights under my belt. But on the other hand, I know I'm tough—I just have to find a way to prove it. I am certain that I have it in me to go really far with this, but I also know there's a long road ahead. Dad is serious and quiet. But his heart is 100 percent in this now, and waste of time or not, he and I are now locked in an unspoken pact. We settle into the silence of the passing scenery, the two of us lost in our own blend of fantasies and fear.

* * *

For being the renowned championship fighter and world-class coach that he is, Urijah "The California Kid" Faber has something of a baby face. He looks more like a surfer than an MMA fighter, with his cinnamon skin and the asymmetrically perfect dent in the center of his chin. At five six, he's no giant, but he makes up for it with crazy agility, physical strength, and evolved mastery. From the moment that I walk into his gym, I understand that I'm in the presence of greatness.

Dad and I take a few wrestling and sparring classes, both of which blow my mind. I can feel the difference in the levels of the teachers and coaches here. It's a cut above everywhere else I have been. I'm physically and mentally cracked open to a new way of doing things, with more style, each movement more dignified somehow. After the class, Urijah comes over to my dad and me.

"You folks live close by?"

"Reno," my dad says.

"Reno? You've come a long way." Urijah sounds surprised.

"I want to train with the best," I chime in.

"You want to join my team? Team Alpha Male?" Urijah asks, as if testing me. I don't answer, and he continues. "Not just anyone can join my team," he says, ping-ponging his gaze from my dad's eyes to mine. "You have to have certain criteria." More eye contact with both Dad and me.

Urijah invites us to sit down and pulls out a piece of paper, on which he strikes a yellow highlighter through a long list of all the different classes that will be required of me to join the team. "If this is what you want, this is how you do it," he says. I love the seriousness behind his words.

Urijah takes what I already know, whatever exists in my mind and in my body, and he pushes me to the next level of possibility. He compels me to chase the breakthrough. In the last few gyms where I trained, I was always somehow on my own, or brushed off. The coaches never really invested themselves in me. Besides Ken Shamrock, Urijah is the first coach who really sees me.

"I can see that you're tough, so I know you're going to give it your all when you fight—but if you want to go big, you need experience," he advises. "You need to train at the highest possible level, with the most intensity you can muster. It's full-on beast mode, or nothing." He runs one of the most prestigious MMA training facilities in the country, in the world maybe, so I feel great about being in his care. From day one, he knows I'm after the very thing he can help me obtain. He gets excited about it, which gets me even more excited about it.

Dad can feel it, too. He's not one to show too much excitement about anything, but his eyes are wide open and he nods along to what Urijah says. We both know it: this is the kind of place I need to be. "Welcome to your new home," Dad says on our way out. We both loved being there, the vibe somehow different and more advanced than anywhere else. There was something cutting edge about it, progressive, too: the teachers all come from different corners of the world, offering up serious mastery in their respective fields. We just needed to iron out the logistics. If I would train with Urijah, I'd be looking at a four-hour commute round-trip through the mountains, and for it to mean anything, I'd have to train at least five times per week. *You belong here*, my instinct whispers. But my logic has the other ear: *Training in Sacramento is insane. Why go through the trouble?* But it's not just about the gym. It's about mentorship. It's about leadership. It's about community. It's about having a home. As crazy as it is, every cell in my body says it's exactly what I need to do.

Yes, the drive sucks, but I start to look forward to it because I know I'm going to come back stronger, more aware, more developed. In the car, I turn up the music loud and think about fighting, and about how much fun it is. I love everything about my situation. Team Alpha Male has fighters from all over the world, so many different nationalities, races, and ethnicities, everyone united by one common goal: to be the best. I've found my tribe, this vibrant group of fighters and coaches, everyone serious and dedicated, but also inclusive and warm. I'm finally somewhere where I have high-level training partners. I don't just train—now I belong to something.

Breathing DREAMS like air.

—F. Scott Fitzgerald, *The Great Gatsby*

ALPHA FEMALE

Within weeks, the drive up the Interstate 80 to Sacramento is locked in, a whole 130 miles one way from our place in Reno to the gym in Sacramento. The four-hour commute is tough, especially when there is snow in the mountains, but it's worth it. I feel myself becoming a beast. My stamina is high, I am becoming more technically advanced, my skill set is broadening. There's a fire in me and fighting is stoking it. Urijah is pleased with my progress, too. Just like I've found solace and inspiration in his care, I feel that he, too, has a real stake in seeing me succeed.

Being a part of Team Alpha Male helps me understand that MMA isn't just about getting into a cage and fighting. To be good—*really good*—you have to possess an arsenal. The truly excellent MMA fighter is a multifaceted multitasker, a wide-ranging expert.

It's called mixed martial arts for a reason. You not only have to know *how* to box, grapple, and throw, but you also have to master all of these things. It's the reason why so many MMA fighters are able to compete well in so many different sports. They're inherently versatile. Anderson Silva, for example, is known to be one of the most diverse martial artists of our generation, holding multiple black belts in tae kwon do, judo, Muay Thai, and Brazilian jujitsu, as well as a yellow rope in capoeira. I get it. If I want to be taken seriously, I have to diversify. I hang on to every single one of Urijah's words, as if he is handing over an ancient recipe for success.

But expenses start to pile up even though I live at home. There's the gas money, obviously, but I'm also spending quite a bit on gear and my phone bill, and there's the need for basic spending cash. I start teaching ballet and tap dance classes at a studio in Reno to generate some income. I'm there two days per week, and the rest of the days my body and brain are in Sacramento, cultivating my arsenal. At the end of some training sessions I'm so physically and mentally drained that I can't fathom getting into a car and driving for two hours.

One day, while I am taking my jujitsu class, I notice my phone buzzing with a text. When I look, I see two missed calls, as well as a text from that same caller saying he or she is trying to get in touch—the latter of which seems odd because I don't recognize the number and the tone of the text suggests that I should. The first thought that comes to me is Seth. I take a small bit of pleasure knowing that if Seth were to show up again in my life now, I could probably kick the shit out of him. But that asshole is capable of anything, so I think twice before calling or texting back. I decide to do nothing. One hour passes. Two. Three. I can't help it—curiosity finally gets the best of me. I want to know who it is. I lock myself in the bathroom and quietly press "Call Back."

"Hello?" It's a man's voice.

"Hello . . . May I ask who this is? I missed a call from this number," I say.

"Oh yes, hi. Am I speaking with Paige VanZant?" the voice asks.

"You are," I say quietly, still reluctant.

"Hi, Paige. This is Dana White."

My skin goes hot, my heart starts to race, and my palm suddenly feels wet around the phone at my ear. Getting a personal call from the likes of Dana White, the president of the Ultimate Fighting Championship himself. Thanks to my dad's obsession with MMA, I've known who he is since I was a little kid.

"Are you sure?" I ask, unable to fathom the truth, and a little irritated that anyone would want to mess with me like this.

"Yeah, I'm pretty damn sure," he says, chuckling now. "I've chosen you to compete in *The Ultimate Fighter*, a reality TV show produced by the UFC, where fighters are split into teams and compete for the chance to officially join the UFC. Does this sound like something that interests you?" I crumble to the floor, clutching my phone at my heart, incapable of grasping his words. A chance to join the UFC is every MMA fighter's dream. This cannot be happening.

When I tell Mom, she cried and tells me she's proud of me, but she doesn't want me to get my hopes up. "Just don't get too excited until you know for sure," she says over the phone. Dad doesn't say anything. I wonder what he thinks. And sure enough, days pass without even a peep on my phone. I start to think Mom might be right. Why would Dana White call *me* out of nowhere? But soon enough, I get a follow-up call from his office. It's true, he wants me on the show. In the end, this is bittersweet in and of itself because I also realize that at nineteen, I'm still too young to participate— you have to be at least twenty-one, since alcohol is served in the house where the fighters live. It's like having the most amazing opportunity of your career dangled out of reach in front of you. I'm crushed, pissed, and energized all at once.

"It's OK," Dad says. "At least you're in Dana White's orbit now. That's not nothing."

And Dad is right, because shortly thereafter, I receive an envelope. I quickly tear it open—it's a four-fight UFC contract.

I may be too young for the TV show—but I'm apparently old enough to be a professional fighter. This is huge. To put it in perspective, this is like getting an NFL contract. This could very well be the single most exciting moment of my career . . . my life even.

I can't afford a lawyer, so I comb through the agreement on my own, doing my best to decipher the legal lingo. I don't understand every little detail, but I know enough to seize an opportunity like this one, and I sign it that very same day. It's a four-fight contract that lays out the terms for how I'll make money when I fight with the league. I earn when I fight. The more I win, the more often they'll try to re-sign me. The letter also lets me know that I will be one of eleven women in a new category called the strawweight division. I don't know the other fighters in the division personally, but what I do know is that they all have way more fight experience than I do. But I don't care. I'm going after it. This is beyond a game changer. It's a life changer.

"I'm impressed, but not surprised," Mom says sweetly. "You were always a tough little thing." I can't imagine what it must be like for a mother—even my mother, who is married to a die-hard wrestler—to live with the reality that her kid will get physically attacked for a living. She seems genuinely happy and terrified at the same time, which I guess is to be expected. And as for Dad, UFC contract or not, his veneer of stoicism never lets up. I know he's excited; he silently roots for me.

I have my first fight contract, and my first fight is months away. Now that I'm signed with the UFC, my name is out there. I need to live up to it. The first order of business is to set up my fight camp, which I decide to do at Team Alpha Male, despite the distance and commute from Reno. It's annoying, but I'm used to the drive by now, and there's no better place to set up than at Team Alpha, where the classes are more advanced and high level than anywhere else I've been. Fight camp is essentially the place a fighter designates as his or her training base for a period before the fight. It also refers to the five- to six-week period before a fight that is focused and extreme, in which the ultimate goal is to get the fighter in the best possible shape, conditioned optimally for the fight, crisp in her movements, and armed with a dynamic range of refined MMA tools. When fight camp starts, the clean diet starts, and there is no time off. During fight camp, there is total devotion and unflinching strictness.

Urijah lays out what I should eat. It's a lot of healthy fats, lean protein, plant protein, fresh vegetables, and lemon water. No cheat meals. No alcohol. No dairy, unless it's yogurt. And definitely no sugar—not even from fruit. This is about getting as lean as possible, by replacing any trace of fat with muscle, some kind of BMI nirvana.

Urijah also sets me up with the best coaches in his gym. I train so hard my body feels like it's going to break. The goal is two-fold: for me to get as strong and fast as possible overall, but to also advance each of my individual MMA skill sets and techniques. In this way, fight camp feels like a personal Olympics—I'm training in Brazilian jujitsu, Muay Thai, wrestling, and boxing separately. For my cardio, I run for miles every morning and do crazy punching bag workouts that leave me so breathless I can't speak a full sentence after I'm done.

As we get closer to the fight, some of the training sessions are structured like MMA fights themselves—as five distinct rounds—with the goal of integrating as many of the different fight elements in those short bursts of time, and so I can start getting used to these short bursts of fight periods.

With Urijah's help, I also start to work with two professional managers, Mike and Jeff at MMA Inc., who take care of all my official MMA business and help create ways for me to gain access and exposure. From scheduling and media appearances to sponsorship opportunities, these guys have my back. For the first time, with Urijah and now Mike and Jeff, I feel like I have a proper fight team. I feel fully supported. When my car breaks down in Sacramento one day, it is Mike who comes to my rescue. These people become family.

My new managers want me to get my head around what it means to fight in a UFC cage. They give me two tickets to watch a fight in Sacramento, and of course I take my dad. We set off on the now very familiar drive through the mountains to get there. I don't even know who is fighting. What I *do* know is the feeling in the space, the excitement in the air, the energy of the crowd, the adrenaline pumping in both corners, the theatrics of the whole thing. I love it. Dad stares into the octagon the whole time, his eyes fixed, his heart rapt. I wonder if he's proud. After all, this is the guy who told me to not bother coming home as a teen unless I'd bloodied up my bully. I allow myself to enjoy that thought as I watch the fight go down.

I try to stay focused and forward thinking. I block out the possibilities of injuries. I know they can happen, and I know they can be severe and even life threatening. There's no getting around the fact that fractures, concussions, and knee injuries can be no joke. I hear about one fighter who got knocked out in practice so hard that he suffered a life-changing concussion. He gets dizzy and he has problems sleeping—and worst of all, he'll never fight again. I know bad things can happen, but I have to keep my awareness on my strength and have faith. Mom rightfully worries about these types of things.

"You can do this," Dad says. "You're tough. You're the only girl on Team Alpha Male, you're a UFC fighter. Go get it."

One morning while training in Sacramento, I feel a shooting pain through my whole spine, and pins and needles at my fingertips and toes. Something is wrong with my back. Unfortunately, it's not the first time I have felt it—it's a recurring injury from my dance days as a kid, when I was told by a doctor I suffered back disk regeneration. I had felt traces of it again in Las Vegas, and I'd thought it was just a fluke, maybe associated with stress. But here it is again, this time burning up my entire lower spine. Any movement I make increases this pain, which feels electric between the bones. I can barely get up off the mattress. I grab my phone, which is luckily nearby, and call my dad, who is on his way to work.

"It's already seven thirty a.m. You're at the gym, right?" is how he answers.

"Dad, I can't move. My back is hurt. I don't know what to do."

"You need to get to a doctor, that's what."

But I don't have health insurance in California. I'll have to drive home. I'm supposed to keep a strict routine to prep for the fight, so I can't afford any sudden schedule detour. This is a setback. I'm crushed. What if I can't fight?

Driving back home, I try to put things into perspective. My back thing isn't new; I shouldn't act so surprised or enraged. I do, after all, lead a rigorous physical life. A recurring back injury is just something I'm going to figure out how to wrangle in the context of my budding career.

The injury humbles me. It reminds me of the innate fragility of my own body. It highlights the irony of being a violent fighter, yet being taken down by something as quiet and passive as a slipped disk in my back. I suppose when you train so physically hard and push yourself in fights to such extremes, you forget that despite it all, you're still flesh and bone.

Between the many visits to a chiropractor and a physical therapist, I learn that I have not one but three herniated disks in my lower back. I'll need to spend hours upon hours stretching my spine out. The therapist gives me a list of exercises to work on every day. I'm meant to do some with his help and some on my own at home. All of them are excruciating.

"You're going to need at least six to eight months of this," the therapist says, cracking his own neck while he talks. "And you'll have to take it easy in training. I'll have to vet all your exercises to make sure they're even safe for you to do. In six months, we can talk about your fight." Murphy's law. Just when I feel the momentum surging, with my first UFC fight so close, this injury has to flare up.

"Don't worry," Urijah says on a call, calming me. "Worst case, we can ask them to postpone it." This makes me feel slightly more at ease. "The most important thing is for you to be healthy, so do whatever it takes to get there." I begin to make peace with reality and start strategizing how to overcome it.

Even though I am attached to Team Alpha Male, I decide to train in Reno. It's where I live and where I'll be doing all the physical therapy. With my lower-back injury, it just doesn't make any sense to drive four hours through the mountains. If I want to heal, I need to be practical. I will have to make do with the coaches at the local gym—and who knows how much I'll be able to train anyway?

When I'm at the gym it's a push-pull between the extreme pain I feel in the lower part of my body and the ferocity with which I want to throw strikes with my fists and elbows. I want to break through the pain so I can move onto winning this thing.

"Go easy," the trainer says one day while I'm doing a set of deep squats.

"Nothing good comes easy," I say, wincing through the pulsing, electric pain that's standing in the way of me and my first fight. The more physical therapy I do, the better I start to feel. Gradually, I start to heal. And the less pain I feel, the harder I start to work at the gym.

My injury gives me even greater respect for the human body. I start treating my body with even more care, eating right, resting more. Being a fighter means my body is my tool. I have to keep it optimized.

"I'm ready to fight," I tell my managers. "Let's go to war." And with that, the fight is back on the calendar and I'm back to fight camp insanity.

And then the hate mail comes. I should have known. How could I not have known that the stubborn demons of the past would soon awaken and come slithering toward me again? And of course, here they appear right when I feel weak. How could I have been so naive as to think stuff like this ever really goes away? This particular piece of hate mail comes in the form of an image of me photoshopped awkwardly with one of my opponents, the words "real fighter" under the opponent's name, the word "garbage" beneath mine. I can't help but wonder if this ridiculousness has any connection to the girls who threw garbage at me in high school. A younger me would crumble just thinking about this stuff. But now I understand how nasty the power of envy can get. I don't hate the haters—they fuel me with more passion.

*   *   *

With four weeks left until my first UFC fight, the most important thing is that I make weight twenty-four hours before the fight, as fighters get weighed by doctors in this very official and sometimes public way. Making weight is how fighters shed pounds quickly before a fight to meet the criteria of their specific weight class. As a strawweight, I have to come in at 115 pounds.

Cutting weight sucks; it's one of the most physically intense things I have ever done. There's a very precise science to it, the goal being to be on-weight for the shortest period of time and still somehow not be the smaller fighter. I have to work with a nutritionist to maximize nutritional density against caloric intake. It's a lean, clean protein regimen with lots of vegetables, absolutely zero sodium, and two gallons of water every day. No prepared foods, no milk, no dairy, no bread. Even though it's a lot of water, I feel dehydrated all the time. The restrictions are so abrupt that I sometimes feel faint or have a hard time hearing. For men, cutting weight seems to happen more smoothly, but this hits me like a Mack truck. I read somewhere that medical experts believe that losing more than 5 percent of your body weight in water is considered unsafe, that it can make your organs shut down, and I'm losing double or triple that to make weight for this fight.

The night before I weigh in, I'm still four pounds over 115. I have to go extreme if I want to bring that number down in twenty-four hours. Luckily, Alexa is with me and can help. Urijah tells us about this trick to cut the weight fast. It involves me soaking in a lava-hot bath, sprinkled with Epsom salts and rubbing alcohol, for as long as I can handle the heat. When I exit the bath, Alexa "mummifies" me in as many blankets and towels as I can handle, keeping a little window open so she can see my face and make sure I don't pass out. After half an hour, I stand up, and Alexa right away uses a credit card to scrape the sweat coming off my skin from head to toe. It's the effect of a squeegee but on a human, and we laugh the whole time. After a few rounds of that, I finally make weight. *My first UFC fight.*

I start drinking fluids, but not too fast, otherwise I'll get sick. The next morning at breakfast, I start introducing foods back into my stomach. I can't eat the wrong foods or I'll get violently ill. No Hooters fries for this fight.

Now that I'm officially with the UFC and part of the new strawweight division, all the fighters have to show up in Texas not just for the fights, but also for the big marketing events to help promote. We have to autograph posters and chat with fans, and attend a press conference—with me pinching myself the whole time because I can't believe this is my life.

There are certain moments when you step outside yourself and watch the scenes of your experience unfold like little gifts, these mystical fragments of time that you get to self-witness. Such moments sparkle like gems in your personal history. Walking into the octagon for my first UFC fight in Austin is one such moment for me. It is like walking into a realm of new possibility, surged by the promise of my own potential. The crowd is going crazy. I walk in, knowing I have to savor this moment, acknowledging that this is unique and that something special is happening.

My goal is clear: to be the star of the strawweight class and take home the belt. I'm up against a fighter named Kailin Curran. But since I've studied tapes of her previous fights, I have a sense of how she moves. I can strategize my evasions. I start by pressing her hard against the cage, which is how I establish myself, to lay down my toughness; but she uses a knee reap position from her back to sweep me. That's OK—I'm just getting started. I do everything I can to get her off her feet in round 2, which works well: she can't break free. And even when she gets close, I pin her to the cage again with all my force, unrelenting. Then I get another takedown in round 3 and I keep hitting her with decisive sharp punches. She's wilting quickly—I can feel the wave of triumph coming. The referee stops the fight at 2:54 and I am declared the winner. I melt onto the mat, into my own disbelief, feeling the surge of all my efforts coursing through me. I cry through my mouthpiece, my eyes squeezed shut, the roar of the crowd the most beautiful sound ever.

I lay down on the floor and weep, releasing my full weight into what feels like a sacred victory, as my spirit soars through the cage. I can see Mom and Dad sitting in the front row. She's crying. He's got his arms crossed, but there's a half smirk on his face, and his eyes are welled up. Even though our fight was nine bouts before the main event, it wins Fight of the Night and I make history as the second-youngest female in the UFC. Suddenly I'm no longer just a professional fighter—I'm a UFC victor. I have validation. I have a title. I have respect. I also have a $50,000 bonus that comes with the Fight of the Night recognition. This is getting real.

People are paying attention now. I'm officially on the map. The fight wasn't televised, only streamed online. But it goes viral and is trending on social media. Emails come pouring in from people who saw it. *We love you*, some of them say. *You're such a badass.*

You're an inspiration. You're my hero. These words land on me like medicine. I was surrounded by haters for such a long time, and now I have fans. Their comments bubble around in me, exciting parts of me and healing others. Everything feels at once terrifying and therapeutic.

My dad doesn't admit it, but I have never seen him this happy. My career feels like something we get to share. Each win is for both of us, a return to something. It's almost funny how the world of brutality and violence is where the sweetness of a father-daughter bond could flourish. But flourish it does.

The next UFC fight is against Felice "Lil' Bulldog" Herrig, a six-year MMA veteran with an illustrious kickboxing career and tons of fights under her belt. I'm still not totally used to all the ancillary work that comes with these fights, and I again forget to bring a proper outfit to wear at the press conference. All I have is workout clothes with me, so one of the ladies on my management team lends me a dress.

Blond, pretty, and spunky, Felice comes out on the night of the fight wearing a little leopard-print bottom. She's a bundle of tightly packed muscles and looks like she's ready to get down. And this girl is a competition machine—she's been fighting professionally since I was in high school. Of her last six fights, she's won five. She's a big-name fighter who has been defeated only by decision. My dad has flown out to New Jersey with me, we're on the main card on Fox, and it's a Saturday night—a constellation of high-stakes variables that inspires even more hustle from me. The face-off is almost surreal, the two of us at exactly 115 pounds, at around the same height, blond braids woven flat down the sides and backs of our heads. Both of us are relentlessly scrappy and hell-bent on winning, but there can be only one winner.

Felice is seasoned, and serious—and I'm essentially the new kid. The tension is thick between us. During round 1, I go in hard and totally swarm her. Maybe it's too much too soon, but there's only one goal flashing in front of me: finish her and finish her fast. Now that she knows what I'm made if, in round 2 I really attack. Even when I fall to the ground, I snap back up. I go in and get her in a clinch and I wrestle her up against the cage. She may have taken my back quickly, but once I'm up I have control of the fight. I get her down and unleash a barrage of ground-and-pound strikes to her face. I scramble faster than she does, with zero lag time in my movements, all pace and pressure, and I never relent. She's a more experienced grappler, but so far, I'm dominating her. In round 3, I batter her with hammer fists, which is when you strike an opponent with a clenched fist, using the side of the hand or wrist. After a grueling fifteen-minute fight, I win with a clean sweep on the scorecards. I prove that what she has in experience, I have in resilience. One of the commentators refers to it as "a changing of the guard" moment in UFC history. Even Dana White tweets, "Paige VanZant is a badass!!!! So young and fights her ass off."

I don't know what's happening, but I love it. I love winning. I love the mastery, the confidence it all inspires, the fact that it's so high stakes and crazy and wild. I love how it forces me to contend with my own badassery, that it doesn't have time for weakness. I love the people. I love their commitment. I love the respect.

I love the freedom in the cage to release the beast within myself and tear someone up as a means to victory. I have to keep going.

The next fight happens in the fall, against Alex "Astro Girl" Chambers, an Australian fighter who is a whopping fifteen years older than me. I am being called a rising star and people argue more and more about whether I deserve or have earned it. I thought that winning fights would make it easier for me, but in reality it raised everyone's expectations for the next fight, and the attention and stress are raised as well. Since it's in Las Vegas, my friend Alexa is with me, to help me prep. She's been down the making-weight rabbit hole with me before, so she well knows that the twenty-four hours prior to a weigh-in can get really weird. I'm a couple of ounces over 115 again, so we have to get creative.

"I know what to do," Alexa says decisively. "Strip down." She disappears into her toiletry bag. I take off my clothes and she comes back with a pink Daisy razor and a bottle of shaving cream. "I got this," she says, lathering my arms and legs with foam and shaving all four of my limbs down to newborn-baby softness. I get on the scale again. Still a few ounces over. She disappears back into her bag of tricks, and this time comes back with a pair of scissors. She wraps me in towels. "Sit." Then Alexa combs my hair and without asking or thinking or second-guessing or even running it by me, she starts snipping off chunks of my hair. "We gotta do what we gotta do," she says. And sure enough, after this impromptu grooming, the two of us cracking up like a pair of hyenas, my weight is on point, and Alexa once again wins at making everything perfect.

The MGM Grand Garden Arena in Vegas is as dramatic a venue as one can imagine. There are seats as far as the eye can see. Fighting here is like fighting on one of the main stages of the world. Now that I have a few of these fights under my belt, there are certain things that I know about myself. Number one: I like to set the tone for the fight. I like to let it be known with crystal clarity that my aggression in the cage is limitless, and that despite my smile and sweet green eyes, I am at war. During the first round my tempo is so quick she can't really keep up with me. My attitude is forward-pushing the whole time. When I have her in a clinch, I go at her with hard knees and strikes. I wear her down. This goes on for another two rounds, to no avail for her, and then in the third round, I drop her and go at her with a ground-and-pound battery, which is when you take the dominant position—it can be on top, in a half mount, or standing in your own guard—and unleash a fury of elbows, punches, forearm strikes, or all of the above. I use this position to achieve an arm bar, which is an arm lock that hyperextends the elbow joint, and which causes her to tap out, at 1:01.

"You did it again!" Alexa screams, squeezing me after the fight, ignoring my stink and all the sweat on my body. I cry and laugh at the same time, every one of these wins feeding into my growing obsession with victory.

"I know! This is crazy!" I say, now throwing myself in the arms of my Team Alpha Male coaches.

"And that girl is a lot older than you, with tons more experience," Urijah reminds me. "You can do anything, Paige. The word we need to focus on now is 'limitless.'"

I begin to move through life with more confidence. I drop into this flow of progress. It feels so good to make money doing something that I love, something I'm good at, something that means something to me beyond just being a sport. It feels good to step into the realness of this space where life is thought through and methodical, organized, and disciplined. It feels good to surprise people, to shock them, to silence the naysayers. It feels good to get stronger, savvier, more serious, to ride a wave of positivity that starts with my very own efforts. Dad comes to all my fights and says nothing. Even though his presence and company feel great, I wish he'd just once say, "Hey, I'm proud of you." Or maybe I have it all wrong, and it's precisely his stoic silence that pushes me to go harder. I suppose I both love and hate him for it. Mom doesn't come at all—it's too much for her, which is fine, because nervous energy is the last thing I need in the cage.

My email inbox is suddenly out of control. There is a mountain of messages to get through, as well as countless voice mails. Journalists, reporters, and photographers are calling all the time. I get lots of requests for interviews and photos, and my managers help me sift through them and decide which ones to take. I see how quick these writers are to angle the conversation, to spin my story in whatever way they please. People want to know my story. They almost can't believe I exist. I duck and dodge their attempts and stay strategic about driving the interviews. I won't have anyone dig indiscriminately into my past.

With so many media requests and fights cooking on the horizon, my managers don't want me to become overwhelmed. They try to strike a balance between pacing things and stoking the fire.

We all feel the momentum, but we need to make sure I don't burn out. But then Reebok calls, and the sponsorship opportunity it offers catalyzes everything. Collaborating with a giant like Reebok puts me on the map in a very public way; but more important, it affords me the chance to finally live and train in Sacramento full time. I don't even care about what the apartment looks like, or how big it is, or if it's furnished or not. I just need a room to rent where I can throw down a mattress and sleep on it when I need to. I find a cheap, empty room in a small, gritty apartment complex in downtown Sacramento. I sleep on the floor there sometimes when I'm too tired to do the drive back to Reno. Some mornings I wake up with the grain of wooden floor embossed onto the flesh of my cheek, but I pick myself up, thank God, smile, and hustle on. I feel so blessed for the opportunity. It feels like my dreams are starting to come true.

I get myself a job doing the night shift of membership sales at a 24 Hour Fitness, which is perfect, because it leaves my day open to train. I don't buy any furniture or make any friends in Sacramento, but I'm not seeing any of that right now. My focus is to train at Team Alpha Male. I go to bed early and eat by myself. I have a purpose and lock into the goal.

My Reebok deal is quickly embroiled in controversy. One journalist writes that "Reebok must love blondes." Apparently, people think I'm still too much of a rookie to have the deal at all, and when I make the mistake of posting a flirtatious video of myself wearing items from the Reebok line I'm endorsing, a

Twitter storm unfurls. Fellow fighters seem particularly scathed, tweeting things like:

Just call 1-800-HOT-GIRL and talk to real live girls.
We can't frickin wait to answer your call. Call now!

The whole thing is eerily reminiscent of when I made the cheerleading team in eighth grade and pissed off all my friends— what as an adult I now know how to identify as good old-fashioned envy. Maybe posting that video wasn't the smartest thing to do— but so what? I'm young, excited about having a deal with Reebok, and social media is a key part of the world in which we live. Mom, being the superwoman that she is, deletes it from my Instagram account before it has a chance to make any more waves. Urijah comes to my defense publicly by saying that it's not about sponsor-ships or anything else; rather, "it's about winning fights."

The truth is, I don't really fit in with the typical girl fight-ers. Most female MMA athletes have been involved in some kind of competitive martial art since they were young. Fighting has been part of their lives and shaped their outlook. Some fighters take on a badass persona, and I'm not sure if it's always real or part of branding themselves. Some are just very focused and seri-ous about fighting as a career, as something they want to dedi-cate their life to. They eat, sleep, and breathe fighting. My point is that most of these women have worked for years, sometimes their entire lives, to get a chance to fight professionally. For me, how-ever, fighting began as an outlet. I didn't grow up wanting to be an MMA fighter. I didn't fight because it was a lifelong goal. It's a way for me to express myself, to celebrate the gifts I have, and to show myself and the world that I am strong. That I can take care of myself. That if you put me in a fair fight, I can find a way to win.

"Do you think you have an easier time as a fighter because of your appearance?" a female journalist asked me one time after a fight.

"I think my opponents always underestimate me," I responded. "But I don't think it has anything to do with the way I look." The next day, the headline reads "Paige VanZant Says She Gets Underestimated Because She's Hot." Around this time, one of my opponents posted an image of a decapitated Barbie doll tagging me, its head replaced with a photo of her own face, with a little note that reads, "Maybe I'll get a Reebok deal now!" Luckily, the opportunity to properly knock her out soon presents itself in a fight.

GO AHEAD,
UNDERESTIMATE ME

I t's UFC Fight Night 80 at the Chelsea Cosmopolitan in Las Vegas, a well-known mixed martial arts event. Our fight is the main event. I have six wins on my résumé, and I'm not backing down for my seventh. Because the strawweight division is new, I can be a world champion. The momentum has been building so much that it feels like Christmas, my birthday, and New Year's all rolled into one. I'm twenty-one, I'm fighting with the UFC—my life is starting to feel like a sort of cosmic arrival. I settle in with myself, attuned to a path of growth, unwavering in my goals. Having such clear focus and direction gives meaning to every single day: I exist to evolve. And my intention feels volcanic. I walk onto the octagon buzzing with a full-body excitement. I'm up against Rose "Thug" Namajunas, who was in *The Ultimate Fighter* and got her feet wet as a taekwondo black belt and jujitsu master all before the age of ten. Taekwondo is a Korean martial art with a strong emphasis on head-height kicks and jumping and spinning kicks; whereas jujitsu is more ground game. This means Rose is primed on every possible level, ready for any and all angles of attack. She's the number three UFC contender in the world and by far a more technical fighter than I am. Rose is beautiful, with her perfect Lithuanian facial structure and pool-blue eyes, an infectious smile, and a gorgeous head of hair—which she shaves defiantly right before our fight. *It's a fight. Not a beauty pageant*, she tweets, her freshly buzzed cut featured on social media.

She takes me down during the first round and batters me with sharp elbows to the face. This girl is strong. My blood tastes warm in the spaces between the mouth guard and my teeth. The gash on my cheek is so bad it's not just bleeding, it's gushing.

"Keep breathing," my coach says as he slathers globs of Vaseline onto the cut to stop the bleeding, to no avail. "You're doing great. You have to stay mean for this one." There's so much blood in my eyes and ears I may as well be fighting underwater—everything is muffled and blurry. When we're on our feet she throws sharp, bullet-like punches, beyond my guard. None of the clinch takedowns I typically use are working on her. And as much as it stings to say it, she's a step ahead of me the whole time. It feels like Rose is in a whole other league of expertise, which might be a result of the fact that I was initially meant to fight Joanne Calderwood, who was forced to pull out five weeks ago and was replaced by Rose, who is currently destroying me. I'm reminded of Dad's warning that having heart is just one piece of the puzzle.

Mastery of skill is the other piece, and Rose has got it on lock. I'm feeling defeated even before I lose.

In the next round, she gets me into a rear-naked choke so tight I have to remind myself to relax my throat, to take small sips of air through my nose, but I start seeing black spots and feel dizzy. Through a sliver of visibility, I catch a glimpse of the giant screen where the fight is projected and see myself, drenched in my own blood, my eye sliced open. I linger there in that zombie state for a moment and ask myself, *Am I done?* And still, I don't tap out. I survive the choke and the battery of fists that follow and when the horn blows, I'm as surprised as everyone else in the room that I'm not actually dead. I may not have the winning hand here, but I am calling up every drop of force I have to prevail.

By the fourth round, she already has six takedowns. Now she comes at me with not one but two deep arm bars, but miraculously, I manage to rotate my wrist and slither out from under her—both times! She takes me down a seventh time. And an eighth time during the fifth round. And it's during this round that she gets me into a rear-naked choke with such a grip that there's no resisting the pressure on the bones in my throat. It is quite literally a life-or-death moment. And so I tap out and Rose wins by submission. The commentators call it the win of her career. At the press conference after the fight, I sit there all busted up and choke back tears. I ask my parents to leave because if they stay, I'll bawl the whole time. I hold myself as strong as possible, but the disappointment burns in me.

It's my first UFC loss and it feels like a little death. I hate losing more than I love to win, so when it happens, I have to mourn it, take it in and get my head around the lessons it came to teach me. And while the loss against Rose feels like a living hell, I discover that my grit during the fight did not go unnoticed. The fight commentators and media even say that while everyone remembers Rose's technical skills, they also remember my tenacity. In this way, I lost the fight but I won the respect of the MMA community. I keep reminding myself that this means something.

One of my teammates, Chad, has a fight that night after mine. I am meant to go, but I just don't feel up to it. I want to lay in bed and just be quiet and still. I want to replay things in my mind. I want to cry. But my mom quickly snaps me out of it.

"Get up," she barks sweetly. "You gotta show up for your people. Now put your big-girl pants on and go handle this," she says, and rips the hotel room blanket off me. She makes a good point, so I pull myself together and get out there, one foot in front of the other, even though my heart is totally broken. That night I post a selfie of my busted face:

"Failure defeats losers but inspires winners. I'll be back. That's a promise."

I clean blood out of my ears for the next three weeks and Urijah and I have long talks about what I did wrong. We talk about how to improve my stand-up and ground game, and how to evolve my whole style to make it even more dynamic. The more apt I am to attack from as many positions as possible, the better. When I'm on my feet, I need to be quick—and when I'm down on the ground, I need to be relentless in my use of pressure.

"You were predictable," he says, not mincing words. I feel a pain surge through my stomach. I can't handle his criticism, but it's true. I hate the feeling of not being good enough. In this moment, I'm on the polar end of the feelings of a fighter. I sit silently to take my beating, wishing I could turn and go home. "You relied on familiar strategies from your last three UFC fights. She knew what to expect!"

"But if I'm good at something, shouldn't I rely on it to win?"

"No—in this game, your unpredictability is akin to your strength."

He makes me understand that a key piece of the game is to keep it fluid. It's like jazz: for it to be any good it has to be a little different each time.

One day I get a tweet from someone named Mark Ballas, who I learn is a *Dancing with the Stars* contestant. "You want to be my dance partner on the show?" he's asking, which is at once one of the most random and amazing things that has ever happened to me. There are few things in life that bring me as much joy as dancing, and honestly it's a piece of myself that feels like it's been buried for years. Dancing might not only be fun, but also incredibly therapeutic. I tweet Mark back saying that I'd be down and send him contact information for Mike and Jeff. I figure that since I'm required to take time off for a short period—known as medical suspension from the UFC—why not?

I love fighting, of course, but there's something exciting about the chance to open myself up to more. It's a piece of luck that nudges me to keep designing a life, a life filled with the unexpected and glittered with what I love. Maybe this is how happiness works, I think: we keep moving forward, keep populating our purpose in new ways, keep expanding beyond what we've imagined. Dance was another opportunity to fill my hours with activities that bring me joy. To evolve both inside and outside the cage. So of course I accept the invitation to appear on *Dancing with the Stars*, at once shocked and overjoyed.

I don't watch the show religiously, but I know it's a big deal. I'm flown to LA to meet with the producers for a sit-down interview. I give my all because that's the only way I know how to do. If I win the show's prize money, it could change everything for me. It would allow me to focus on my MMA training, and I'd never have to worry about side work. I could pay off loans, help my parents; I could even save and start looking toward the future! Up until this moment, I've been focused on the present: winning and then getting the next fight. This opportunity allows me to think bigger.

Two whole months go by and I hear nothing. I try to manage my expectations by not thinking about it, but since I'm on a required break from fighting, for those two months the *Dancing with the Stars* fantasy is pretty much *all* I can think about. The ruthless competitor in me is officially intrigued, she who sees everything as a sport, all things in the context of power. Two weeks later I get the call—*I'm in*! I'm again flown to LA, where I'll be based for the season.

My dance partner, Mark, and I click from the start. He seems to know what I am made of even before we hit the floor; he already knows something about the way we're going to move. Our personalities gel nicely: we're both serious and hardworking, but we know when to goof off, too. He reeks charisma in every single number and leads with the crisp precision of a pro regardless of the genre. For two weeks straight, we practice intensely for our first routine. I plan to hit that stage floor with unadulterated passion. I came to do this.

I treat our practice studio like I treat the cage: a place to give it my all. To call on every shred of talent and ability I have and channel it in the direction of a win. I apply my fight work ethic to rehearsing. I don't complain and I don't take breaks. But unlike fighting, dancing feels like an anatomical vacation, a physicality that's free of violence, led mostly by exhilaration and the sweetness of song. On the dance floor, we're in it together, a cocreation of movement; whereas in the cage, it's each woman for herself. As dancers, we feed and support one another's movements; in the cage, it's all-out war. Even though it's odd at first, I allow myself to enjoy this break from the innate brutality of my career. I slip into the whimsy of dance, the gliding and flow. I even enjoy the many hours of hair and makeup and wearing costumes and connecting with the feminine parts of myself that are usually not in play. The theatrics of each number excite me, the sets, the sparkles, the character shoes, the warm-ups, the stretching, the sweat. It is in this world of dance that I allow myself to relax into the sensual.

I start to understand myself even more, by realizing that I've always been drawn to these deep, immersive experiences—that I am *experiential* by default. That I love to throw myself into the heart of a challenge and wring myself out trying to work through it. That I'm a learner. That I am intoxicated by challenge. That I am really content only when I am pushing my edges. That I take pleasure in the tension of the competition, finding my joy in the tiny crevices between good and great. That I love being around people like this, like-minded doers who show up to win. That every opportunity to perform reconnects me with my essence.

Our days revolve around the rigors of a schedule that includes learning and practicing lots of choreography. Sometimes we practice for so long we forget to have lunch and training becomes a vortex of chasing perfection. The producers need their narratives, too, which means they try to angle our stories at their own discretion. Even though we are there to dance, they seek peepholes into our humanity, cracks beneath our glitzy costumes.

"So, Paige. As a tomboy, you probably hate all this girly-girl stuff that's required on the show," one of the particularly fast-talking producers says—not *asks*—during a talking-head interview one day. She smacks her gum and twirls her gel-slicked curls compulsively, and she checks the notifications on her phone like it's a nervous tic.

"No, I actually love the dress-up part of this! And the makeup!" I correct her, just trying to stay true to myself.

"No, but really. You must hate it," the producer insists. "Tell me about that." I giggle a little nervously, but stay steadfast.

"There's nothing to tell—dressing up and wearing makeup is really fun. I get a huge kick out of it." The producer is now practically scowling. Maybe she can't fathom a world in which a tough woman, a professional fighter, can also vibe with getting her hair and makeup done. The whole thing becomes an ongoing negotiation based on what they need versus what we as contestants can stomach saying or doing, and it's not without a fair amount of tension. After all, this is a job and the show producers are our bosses.

At one point during the season, while being questioned by producers, I come out and talk about how I was bullied in high school. I don't say too much more than that, because frankly I don't think it's appropriate for *DWTS*, but I share that little part of myself because I'm starting to feel that by being in the public eye more, I have a platform. Mark thinks we can win this thing if I open up to the producers even more. But I like to earn my victories, so there is no chance in hell I'm going to play the sympathy card. I'm not going to give myself up for a vote—that's just not how I win. So Mark and I arduously work our way through the season, one number at a time, hustling through the insanely fun and serendipitous grind as a team.

Each one of our dances is technically challenging for its own reason. Staying on tempo for some of the routines has almost an Olympic intensity. Sometimes I dance with one partner, sometimes with two, and a few times we're in teams. Many of the sets include big throws, leaps, and a sense of cardio no less demanding than that of my biggest fights. Just as I do in the cage, I drop into it with full trust in the power of my own body. I drop into the certainty that I am made to do this, to be tossed and twirled, to leap and land, to nail the details and to show swag and a smile the whole damn time. Just like when I am in the cage, having this much agency over my anatomy makes me feel like I can do anything.

Since the numbers all have their own genre and style, each asks for a completely different type of immersion. Every choreography is a unique opportunity for me to know even more about my own physical limitations. Each song invites a different aspect of my personality to step up and presents a new sentiment or signature for me to unlock. Moving through the styles, I pick up nuances about the world, about cultures, about gestures, about what it takes to stylize something with a certain flare, what it means to be authentic. Tango is different from salsa is different from waltz is different from fox-trot is different from rumba is different from quickstep, and so on.

The salsa routine demands that I completely free my hips so that my mind can follow the steps. I have to unhinge my pelvis in completely new ways, tapping into the revelation that Latin dance begins and ends with the booty. For the quickstep number, I have to dig for something else—a carefree and happy innocence with which to glide all around the stage. We even do a paso doble number that's meant to simulate a fight, which is at once cool and interesting, but for me also very meta. For the Austin Powers jazz number, I'm all pomp and funk, and I even get to fly for a moment, which takes me back to my cheerleading days—only now I am flying high on national television. For a playful samba piece, I wear a warrior-like tribal costume with my hair in a Mad Max she-mullet, flanked by two partners who are supposed to be peacocks vying for my attention. For the jive piece, which we dance to "Proud Mary," I channel my own blend of Tina Turner, my hair tossed kinky and teased out like a lion's mane, my strong legs featured in a tiny red-fringe minidress. It's a big, high-octane, sexy, give-everything-you-got kind of dance that feels electric between Mark and me and earns us our first perfect score of 10-10-10. In one of our final tango pieces, it's all steaminess and seduction and I dig deep for the woman in me, the master flirt, the temptress—and I have a complete blast doing it. It's one thing to excel with a face full of blood, a mouth guard, braids, and no makeup. But killing it in heels, hair, and makeup, I learn, is equally fun.

During my freestyle dance with Mark to a particularly soulful and live rendition of "Over the Rainbow," I strip off the glamour and I let feeling drive. I reach into my heart and explode into the music. I feel the beauty and sadness of everything, so I let it drive my movements. I don't know if it's the tempo of the song, which somehow feels like a lullaby written to my past, or if it's the innate tenderness of the melody, but for some reason I leave a little piece of my sadness in the performance, and oddly enough, it works.

As the weeks pile up, our days begin to feel like a surreal combination of the Cirque du Soleil and boot camp, a unique obstacle course of theatrics that we have to regularly climb through. I start to understand the rigors of what it means to be in show business, always having to be on, to look a certain way. It may not be cage fighting, but it's hard nonetheless. During the competition, UFC fighters like Chuck Liddell and Tyron Woodley come to my performances; and Joanna Jędrzejczyk, the champion of my division, posts something online showing her support. Even Thug Rose herself is rooting for me online! Some of these people are my competitors in the cage, but still, we're all part of the same tribe. We show our humanity first. And since I belong to not one but two amazing tribes now, after all I've been through with building trust and community, it feels incredible when they overlap. My mom also attends all my shows, and knowing she's out there every time fuels me with adrenaline.

During the season, my mom emails me a link to a story that has come out in the local news featuring a mug shot of my ex Seth and accounts of his past brushes with the law; the story vaguely mentions me. Even though my name itself isn't there, this feels like a kick straight to the ribs. Why can't I just be free of all this bullshit? Why does the past always want to keep pestering me?

"I can't have this story come out now!" I cry to Mark one day during one of our last rehearsals. "We're so close to winning this!"

He puts his arm around me.

"Just focus on the dances—put all your power *there*. Nothing can touch you right now. Not even your past. The you of right now is in charge—and if it isn't, get her up here," he teases. "You ready to crush this thing?" And with that, he hits play on the track and we slide into the trance of dance.

Ultimately, the fact that Mark and I make it to the runner-up position is a testament to a confluence of various things: one, that Mark is one of the most hardworking and intuitive people I have ever met or worked with. Two, that we have insane chemistry on the dance floor and a symbiotic appreciation for one another's physical abilities that expresses itself in every single one of our dances. Three, his choreographies are fire, each one more interesting, sexy, and dramatic than the next. And four, we work our goddamned asses off, day and night.

When we finally do become eliminated, it's against Nyle DiMarco, the hearing-impaired model, who performs a haunting duo performance to a particularly moody cover of Simon and Garfunkel's "Sound of Silence." There's no getting around the power of that moment, the emotional heaviness of a deaf man actually moving (impeccably!) to music he can't even hear, and to a song with a title so eerily relevant. Talk about meta.

During that same finals night, while Mark and I dance our last salsa routine to Pitbull's "Fireball," the sweat drips down the back of my dress as red and orange sequins fly all over the stage. The rhythm of the music feels like fireworks onstage, and at one point it hits me that I don't even care if we win. The fact that we got all the way here feels incredible. Here I am again, showing myself and the people around me that I am capable of anything and everything I pursue.

In the end, the real win on *Dancing with the Stars* has very little to do with the actual competition and everything to do with my mother. Mom not only planted the seed of dance in me long ago, but she really also lived for those early days of hustling me back and forth from shows to rehearsals. She was there to facilitate, assist, support, watch, critique—but mostly she just reveled. She used to love watching me dance, her eyes glossy, following me across the stage, her hands clasped at the base of her neck. I remember catching her eye during some of the shows, witnessing her pride from my spot on the stage, and we lock in that stare, linked on this language of dance, so naturally that it really must be in our DNA. When I dance on the show, I'm really dancing for her.

Reality TV has been a trip. It's been wildly fun, I've earned some cash, met tons of incredible people, and made some wonderful connections. But I miss the rawness of being in a fight, the gnarly immediacy of being cooped up inside a cage. I miss setting up fight camp, of picking my home base and the people who are going to help me achieve the most killer training, and getting in the headspace of a countdown. I miss the energy of a venue in the exact moment when the fighters first walk in, the surge of hope pumping like adrenaline in both corners. I haven't had a fight since my defeat against Rose Namajunas, so I am definitely ready to take back my stats.

On August 27 in Vancouver, British Columbia, I fight "Rowdy" Bec Rawlings, another Aussie. Being in the cage this time, I experience a flurry of emotions. On the one hand, I'm so excited to be back. This is home base, after all. But on the other hand, many people have most recently seen me as a dancer on prime-time TV. For a brief moment, I wonder if it's even possible to still have the full respect and attention of the fight world. This fear compels me to fight with even more fury. In the words of Ken Shamrock, "I will get my respect, or I will die."

My opponent is two inches taller than me, five years older, and covered in tattoos. Her head is half shaved, half braided. I know she's going to come with a high-level boxing game, so I need to be able to handle her range. But I pace myself during the first round and don't rush to close the distance. *Don't be predictable*, I tell myself. I stay on the outside, throwing lots of kicks. Bec stalks me, unleashing her strikes methodically, at her pace. I am initiating much less than I usually do, but it's by design—I don't want to risk getting sloppy so early on. But if I have any intention of wearing this girl out I have to engage more. I have to get her in a cinch. For now, though, let me just dance around her and take her cardio temperature.

I have been practicing some of these moves during training, but I have yet to ever really test them out in the cage. But I have learned from my last fight, and this time I am doing things differently. And during round 2, against the counsel of my coach, I let out another flying head kick, which this time knocks her out, after which I pummel her with full force and the whole thing ends right there. I go wild, animalistic. I scream at the top of my lungs, through the chunk of the mouth guard, tears and sweat blurring into my eyes. That kick was a taste of transcendence. It was one of those moments when it's not even me—it's the spirit channeling through me. I hug and high-five the two Team Alpha Male coaches who were able to be with me, as the crowd roars, most of them standing and clapping, a lot of them dumbstruck. No one was expecting this move out of me. I even earn a Performance of the Night award and a $50,000 cash bonus. It's good to be back.

With some of the money, I decide to buy Mom a new Subaru Outback as a surprise for her birthday. At first I tell Dad and he gives me a hard time, because he thinks I should be smart and save my money. But you know what? It is my money, and I have the right to do it for her. I've worked for it. She's had the same Honda Accord for about twenty years, so it's a family event. When I give it to her she sits in it silently, parked on the driveway and doesn't move a muscle, like it's some kind of altar. I'm not sure she's ever even taken it out.

It's December and I'm set to fight Michelle "The Karate Hottie" Waterson as Fox's main event. We're not part of the lineup—we *are* the lineup. Being on the main card is both thrilling and mortifying. It feels good to be featured, but a loss will be that much more magnified. I don't know much about Michelle other than the fact that she has a serious background in traditional martial arts.

During fight camp, my foot and ankle are injured, which makes training at full speed impossible. I can't afford to put off a fight this important, so I just work through the pain. As the weeks progress and the fight grows closer, my ankle refuses to heal. It's easy to get down when you're injured. It gives you an excuse to slow down, to quit. It opens up my mind to all the doubts and negative voices. *I'm not good enough. I don't deserve to be the main event. I don't belong in the UFC.* It's so frustrating to accomplish so much and, yet, negative thoughts still find a way to creep in. I push through the rest of fight camp, focusing on my purpose. I want to win. I want to provide for my family and my future.

The fight is in Sacramento, my new hometown, my fight camp base, so I can't fail. I have to show Team Alpha Male that they have trained me well. The stakes are crazy: winning tonight can catapult my career—and losing gives her my current position. The pressure is heavy, the feeling that all eyes are fixed on whatever is going to happen next. Like me, Michelle has been modeling from an early age and she's also made her own rounds on reality TV. At the official weigh-in, the two of us break out into a playful freestyle dance-off for fun.

But she takes my ranking and I lose the fight. Right from the start, Michelle clinches me against the cage, closing the distance, and with that she's able to throw me onto the mat. From then on, it's a tussle, but I can feel that my ground game isn't at its max, and she does everything she can to finally sink me into a rear-naked choke. She adjusts her grip, and I can feel my airway closing in, that familiar feeling, it's how I went down with Rose. Here I am again—hanging in the hairline sliver between life and death, pushing myself to endure, sipping air through the stress of it, and plowing forward on the fuel of pure resilience. It feels like the pressure is going to snap my throat, so I tap out and suck in what feels like a gallon of air. I have lost the fight by submission in the first round, which is both a swift kick in the ass and a wake-up call to the fact that I have my work cut out for me.

After a loss like this, I skip the gym for a while but, once again, it's Mom who snaps me back into reality. "If you're serious about actually doing this, you better stay at it," she warns, her tone intent. She sounds the alarm I need to get me up off my ass, working hard again, with my eye on the big picture.

A less experienced me might take a defeat such as this one to heart. Michelle took my position, after all. And while it's true that I hate losing, for some reason I face this loss with a new blend of dignity. I accept it as a reality of my evolution as a fighter. I start to see that there will always be wins and losses and that the real point is to give it my all. It's one thing for me to beat some of the less-seasoned fighters whom I have won against before, but if I want to be a champion, I need a new bar: I need to start finishing the higher-echelon women, the Tecia Torreses, Rose Namajunases, and Michelle Watersons of the world. And for that, I will need more technique, more discipline, and more precision. I'm not mad at that. Bring it all, is my attitude.

I hold a BEAST, an ANGEL, and a madman INSIDE ME.

—Dylan Thomas

GRIT & GRACE

I know it sounds insane, but I decide to move back to Oregon. I return to the source of some of my best and worst hours for the simple reason that I want to define my home state on my own terms. I want to fall in love with it again. But when I try to trace the history of hate that pulsed through major moments of my life here, I always come up short. Sure, I can understand that it happened—I just can't understand why. And in the fogginess of this limbo I make a choice: to choose love. I can't control other people, their way of thinking, or their behavior. What I can do is maximize the agency I have over my own life. And I want to be a lover *and* a fighter.

Sometimes it feels like my life is woven together from the innate duality of everything that comprises it. As a dancer and a fighter, I have to work with rhythm *and* strength, with coordination *and* stamina, with balance *and* brawn. I am very much my parents' daughter—she a dancer, he a wrestler—their legacies of physical robustness entwined in me. I know I'm still young. I wish I could sit that fourteen-year-old me down and say, *Look, your rape was without a question the absolute most evil, horrible thing that has ever happened to you—but it will also somehow be your most important teacher.* Through the years, I slowly peeled back the layers of the trauma, first by admitting it happened, by talking about it, by processing it, and ultimately by crafting an entire identity and life purpose around the notion of self-empowerment. Maybe that's the purpose of pain. To strengthen. To cultivate resilience. To condition. To teach.

I'm in awe of the power within one's self to climb out of just about anything. The power to redefine the terms of our mission in life at any given time, even in the face of the most harrowing rock bottoms. There was a time not long ago when my life felt haunted by a constant darkness, a gash in my soul that just bled and bled. Every day was a wrangling of demons. Now I see the demons less and acknowledge the angels more. Instead of counting down the hours left to sleep, I milk every waking minute. I live. I experience. I feel the fullness of existence in my body and mind, and there isn't a moment that I take for granted, because at one point I wanted to die. The goal is consistent: to stop my inner lamentations dead in their tracks, and any time I feel down, to dig deeper and remind myself to transform the melancholy into might. In this way, for me the act of being a committed fighter occurs all the time, in real time, from the inside out. And those dark gray corners of my memories slowly flood with luminescence and the golden promise of possibility.

Yet I feel the need to keep shedding the calloused pieces of my past. Despite my growth, traces of the agony still linger on me like tiny strips of seaweed that cling to wet flesh after a swim. Unseen to most, sticky nonetheless. I aim to shake them off, but the essence of these emotional pathogens *is* to persist. So there they always are, these prickly little reminders. Sometimes the tiniest things can trigger a memory, like the long pinky nail of the woman who gave me a manicure the other day, and forever the strummed jangle of a ukulele, whose twinkling sound is thought of as sweet to most, but to me is the soundtrack to death. I know these memories will never fully vanish, because experiences such as these seep into the tiniest folds of one's existence. I can blur the thoughts. But I know I can't erase them.

One day, in an act of metaphorical scab-picking, I drive to the Newberg police precinct. I'm not even sure why. Or maybe I am. I just know in some intuitive way that I am supposed to go there. It's been a while, but the thread still pulls.

Pulling into the parking lot, the memories flood back. Just stepping outside the car proves to be tricky for me at first, but I manage and walk up to the entrance. But once I swing open the door of the precinct, everything shifts.

"Paige VanZant! I watched your fight!" a young officer says, pushing back his chair with a loud screech. He stands, and a giant smile of admiration forms across his face. He looks like he might even salute me.

"I'm here to pick up a box of personal items. I left it here a few years ago when I gave my statement. About my rape." The words are crisp as they leave my mouth—delivered with a tone that has nothing to hide. I say the word "rape" not as a victim, but as a survivor. The cop looks at me slack-jawed and dumbfounded, sizing up his understanding of me as a professional UFC fighter in the context of what I just said.

"Of course," he says, his cheeks suddenly flushed. "Let's get you a release." After some phone calls and a fair amount of administrative shuffling, the officer produces a document for me to sign, which will grant me access to my own most private possessions. While he's off doing that I reflect on the fact that I left all traces of these memories here, in the care of the police, during which time I worked on myself, strengthened myself, conditioned myself to be the best that I can. Now strong, I can take back my past.

I open it. Everything is exactly as I left it. Tons of journals and notes from that time, some of them recounting what happened, others just quickly scribbled blasts of suicidal thinking. A written testament of my darkest hours. I can't look at it in front of the cop. I snap the box closed and thank the officer for his help. He congratulates me on my accomplishments and walks me out to my car, even asking for a selfie and my autograph.

I set the box in the driver's seat. I'm not sure where I'm going, but I feel something. I feel the call of my own soul to *do something*. I feel it's time to shed yet another layer.

I arrive at the cemetery where my grandmother is buried. I haven't been to her grave in ages. The earth is damp and spongy beneath me, and on Grandma's grave there is an elaborate regal-looking tangle of moss draped on her tombstone like a green velvet shawl. I sit on the ground with the box in my lap. There is a vast stillness, with the exception of the occasional insect wing flutter or rustle of a leaf. I open the box, the sound of the old cardboard suddenly loud in the silence. I slowly take out one piece of writing at a time, reading aloud the wrath and fury of each one, telling the ghost of my grandmother, the trees, the sky, the grass, the insects, and the flowers about the worst thing that has ever happened to me. Telling this story isn't something I've done that many times in my life—but letting it all go there to nature and the unseen feels oddly more appropriate than my confessions to Alan, the police, Alexa, and Dr. Morgan. Now I release the story to God. I release the words "I was raped," and the heaviness from every etching and every scribble, casting them outside me, watching them fall like dry leaves onto a grave. And like a snake molting old skin, I keep stepping outside the dead parts and slide into the rest of my life.

Non-MMA people are always shocked to hear that I'm a professional fighter, and when they see images of my face all bloodied their eyes go wide. They can't imagine a life of such violence. They can't fathom that one would voluntarily put themselves through that kind of pain. But they don't realize that I have been through so much worse. That I think about my past almost every single day. That in the fading rearview mirror of my experience, I always try to understand. I unravel the moments from each scene, to tease out the causes and effects that became the complex blueprint of my life. I dig through the memories, I trace my steps backward, I try to do the math. And somehow, it always comes back to one simple word:

Hate.

It's a certain blend of hate that turns a bunch of cheerleaders, who, by definition, are supposed to be bubbly, encouraging, and positive, into a pack of conniving bitches. It is also hate that turns a supposed friend into a vicious sexual abuser. It is an awful brand of hive-mind hate that lays the groundwork for the cruelty that follows me throughout my adult life. It's hate when someone questions my skill set or my seriousness about being a fighter. It's pure hate that inspires comments on social media to the tune of "I hope you die." (I mean, I know I'm involved with a violent sport, but who wishes that on someone else? There isn't a fight I go into without first having prayed not only for myself but also for my opponent.) And it's the essence of hate that causes kids in Newberg (long after my time there) to feel so bullied and oppressed that in the span of six months I hear about at least three suicides there; a hate so insanely bad, there are signs up all over that town urging kids to seek help when they feel despair. It breaks my heart to think of my hometown as such a dark hub, but I know exactly how those kids feel. I am those kids.

I was so desperate for company and friendship that I was willing to compromise my own standards. I clung to the idea of belonging, but the groups to which I sought to belong were not particularly interesting or smart. I got older and continued to chase chaos for the wrong reasons. I dated men who tried to oppress me. I drank alcohol to numb myself out. I even tried to kill myself. But when fighting became a real option, *I chose it*. I declared it as my own. I identified something positive for my life and dedicated myself to going after it.

I remember feeling so overcome with despair that I forgot who I was. I sunk into that feeling and drowned inside its power, and in that process the best parts of me became so faded and muted that they finally just switched off. I allowed the sadness to strip me of my own essence. I couldn't help it. It was bigger than anything I could understand, like an emotional tsunami whose very nature was to persist indefinitely. I wish I could have whispered into my own ear, *Please trust me, everything is going to be OK. Your life has meaning. Your path will emerge. Your life is worth it. You are a survivor. You are strong.*

I would tell that younger me, just like I would tell a stranger: Listen, no matter how bleak everything feels, no matter how much you hurt inside every single day, no matter how intensely you feel that you'll never come out of the hole in which you feel trapped, you have to believe there is hope. And even if you don't believe it, find something—for me it was fighting—and let that something be what you live for. Imbue it with intention. Nurture it. Protect it from the parts of you that make you want to give up. Cast it far from the place where you harbor your darkness. Make it the light. Because the more power you give to this special something, whatever it is, the more power it has to lift you out of pain and hurl into purpose.

Just as I believe that fighting was always part of God's plan for my script, I also feel that my script now is about giving back; it's about using my experience, and the lessons that followed, as a tool to support anyone who feels mired in depression. I share my story to obliterate hopelessness. To inspire faith. To help shatter the thick walls of pain that harden around a person's will to go on.

To help melt that down into an energy that can be channeled into something better.

I also share my story for the women (and men) who have suffered (or are still suffering) sexual abuse, for all those victims who are swallowed whole by fear and shame, for the ones who feel they have to stifle the truth and the flood of emotions that comes with it, the ones who live plugged up by their own private hell. The sooner we all learn to talk about these things, horrific as they are, the sooner we can process them. And the opposite is also true: the longer they fester, the longer they take to heal. Even though I was a broken person, for a long time I lived in full denial of what happened to me. Reporting it to the cops was the tip of the iceberg. Talking about it with a therapist, with close friends, and now here with these words, with the concreteness of ink on a page, I declare it all.

By taking this stance, I stand with people like Alyssa, a young fan from New York who read about my bullying and felt a call to rise. One day, I received a private message from her on Instagram, in which she shared details of her private struggle with me. Her honesty moves me, her courage inspires me. I write back right away: *I am here for you.*

We become friends. I even visit her in New York. We go out for pizza. We make each other laugh, reminding one another that beyond even the deepest despair is hope. We write to one another and send gifts on our birthdays. Just by sharing and talking about our pasts and present, we lift one another up. And now that I am in the public eye in a real way and have a platform, I can share these personal motivations with so many others: those who feel held down in their lives, those who are shamed in some way, those who are told they can't do something, those who are senselessly bullied, those who are not taken seriously, and those who want to be the best.

Experience has taught me that life itself is a fight—to win at it, you have to be all in. But to win you must also know when to lean on your tools, your trusted techniques to pull you through the most challenging encounters. Because life will stare you down. It'll try to intimidate you. It'll come at you with its teeth out. It'll try to choke you out. It will grab you and try to slam you down. It will try to hold you in place. It will pin you into submission until you feel like you're going to lose yourself. It'll ground-and-pound you, and it won't care that you're bloody, broken, and on the edge of death.

But you can always rise. You can ignite the part of yourself that chooses life, and compel it to take over. You can scramble out of the worst clinch and take the power back. You can strike back harder. You can come back with an even bigger move. You can return with such a vengeance that you surprise even yourself. It all begins with remembering the basics.

MAKE EVERY MOVE COUNT

The cage, like life, is a chess game, which means you have to stay several steps ahead of whatever you face, knowing that whatever you do now lays the groundwork for what happens next. As in life, you have to pace yourself, observe, choose wisely, and think through your behavior, even the micromoves. And if you do make a mistake—and you will; it's called being human—remember that you can always come back. There is always a path back. Just because you get the shit kicked out of you in round 1, it doesn't mean you're not going to win.

BE DECISIVE

When you're in a fight, there's no time to think—you have to move with your instinct. You have to trust yourself implicitly, trust in the power of your brain and body to deliver what you need to prevail. I wish more adults in my life had been more decisive about helping me when I was in the throes of my most painful moments. When I think back on my life, I wonder whether my first cheerleading coach, or anyone else, could have done anything to change things. What if my coach had intervened? What if she had called my mom? What if she had called the principal? What if, when my mom saw what was happening, she had felt supported and empowered enough to call the coach? What if one grown-up— *any grown-up*—had noticed what was going on and stepped in and said anything at all? When we witness someone else's pain, it's our job to stand up, to speak up, and to be advocates for one another. Everyone's pain is real.

FIND THE WIN IN EVERY LOSS

Losing is my enemy. I hate it with a passion and I hate it more than anything. And yet there will always be losses. Even the greatest athletes in the world suffer losses. But buried in every single loss is a kernel of a lesson that can somehow change your game or take you to the next level. My two losses were some of my greatest performances, and they were ultimately what got me on the radar of many people. You can't let your losses define you; on the contrary, you must use them to catapult you forward. Learning to embrace loss is almost like reaching the enlightenment level of an athlete, this mystical place one has to experience to become a better fighter and human being. Sure, I still feel down about a loss sometimes, but instead of lingering in that fog, I watch it like an episode of something, let it run its course and turn it off.

CHOOSE YOUR CORNERS WISELY

Your "corners" refers to the crew of people you assemble to support and coach you through a fight. You pick your corners mostly based on who is available, but also on the kind of energy that you want to create for yourself in the cage. After all, these are the folks who will hype you up, wipe you down, keep you hydrated and keep you focused; they'll serve as both your medics and your cheerleaders.

Today I choose my squad and loved ones like I choose my corners. I am selective about who I bring into my inner sanctum. It's not that I don't trust people—I just want to surround myself with the best. I ask myself: Who will do whatever it takes to save my life and have my back? Who will stay loyal? Who is with me until the bitter end? I seek individuals who chase things like dignity and righteousness—and I walk away from everyone else. As my collaborators, confidants, and companions, I choose people who are willing to invest in the value of a true human connection. As Ken Shamrock says, "Lions work together as a group—as a pride—to hunt their pray, to overcome, to prevail."

And also with respect to corners, God is always in mine.

MAKE DISCIPLINE YOUR BEST FRIEND

As a fighter, you have to be catlike in your use of force, but monk-like in your approach to discipline. You have to be willing to drop into the intensity of a daily physical regimen not unlike that of the most well-built ancient Greeks. It is the consistency that comes with a steady discipline that fosters growth, that generates change. To master discipline, you must cultivate a deep respect for your schedule; you have to squash idleness and inertia and see every hour as sacred. Embracing discipline means showing up every day, especially on the days when you don't want to.

KEEP THE FOCUS ON YOURSELF

When I'm standing in front of someone whose intention it is to break me in half, I can't help but wonder: *What if she's stronger than me? What if I can't get out of one of her clinches? What if her long legs lock me in on the ground? What if she has more experience than I do?* But here's something crucial I have learned: there will always be someone with more experience and longer legs. So what? There will always be people out there, opponents and otherwise, who will seem to have the upper hand, who will appear to be better poised to get ahead of you. The real task is not to assess all that, but instead to keep the focus on yourself—to shut down the voice that tries to tell you, you are not enough.

BE UNPREDICTABLE

I can't go into the cage and do the same thing every single time, because that would give my opponents the ability to know what to expect from me. To keep winning, I have to show up with new tricks each time. I have to evolve. I have to show my opponent that I have more than one dimension, that I am not just one thing. Life is the same: There's nothing exciting or worthwhile about the status quo. The trick is to keep growing. To surprise even yourself.

CRUSH DOUBT

There are moments when I have trained so hard, done ridiculous amounts of sit-ups and held infinite planks, ran countless miles, swung God knows how many kettlebells, and thrown so many punches onto a bag that I felt my fingers turn blue—moments when it felt like I literally could not take another step. It's at that delicate threshold that I press on. I crush doubt and pull up from a place of possibility. I tell myself that I can. Likewise in the cage. Even when I feel my most insecure, when I am down, when I am pinned, when I am bloody, I say those two words to myself—*crush doubt*—and I move through whatever is happening fueled only with positivity.

MASTER RESILIENCE

One of the things you'll hear almost every commentator say during my fights is, "That Paige is tough." But it's kind of a given to call a fighter tough—we *are* tough, it's our nature. What I think they actually mean is *resilient.* Since I am still early in my career, and still trying to amass experience and develop technique, to stay relevant I have no choice but to rely on my sense of resilience. I have to grit my teeth and handle the pressure. I have to withstand incredible amounts of pain. I have to stay alive. And every time, inside and outside the cage, it is the force of my resilience that keeps me rooted. A gripping, obstinate, unflinching sense of personal stamina. This force tells me, *I will not be stopped.*

ALWAYS LEARN

Every gym, every training session, every sparring partner, every fighter's history, every fight—*everything* has a lesson woven into it, which means that my trajectory as a fighter, and as a person, builds on itself, each moment facilitating the next one. Losing fights teaches me to crack open the case, figure out what I did wrong, and integrate the learning for the next opportunity. By arming myself this way, the next opportunity eclipses the pain of the loss.

LEAD WITH YOUR HEART

When I first started to train, I didn't even watch fights or know anything about the fight world. I had no idea who the players were or what their stories were. I did it because I loved it, for the sake of itself and nothing more. That was my heart driving. I love the life I lead because I do the things I love. Period. Right now, one of the things I love doing the most is making a roast tri-tip. I like to marinate the meat for a long time. Then I do a wet rub and a dry rub. It's a commitment, but I do it because I love it. When you do what you love, you come at it with heart. You transcend the going-through-the-motions-ness of existence and dip into some actual glory. I say scour your heart to find the things that make it flutter, and define goals that are in line with the things that actually mean something to you—*the things that mean the most to you!* Be in love with your purpose. Be a champion of your own dreams.

HAVE THE HEART OF A CHAMPION

Having the heart of a champion means I'm not just here to have fun and make some money—it means I really want to be the very best. It means that no matter what I do, I'm always going to establish straight off the bat that I'm not joking. It means that if I'm going to go to the trouble of doing something, I engage every piece of myself. I use every muscle. I go all in. I am fully present. I don't half-ass. I push hard. I bulldoze through my comfort zones. I meet each day with a built-in willingness to be my best, to over-deliver. I make over-delivering my base point. I exercise enthusiasm. I ritualize my practice. I get animalistic. I go beyond what I think is normal. I chisel toward precision and perfection. I study myself. I study my enemy. I don't spend my days on nonsense. I don't fill my mind with trash. I cultivate confidence at the cellular level.

BE EXACTLY WHO YOU ARE

It excites me to live in a world where gender norms are blurred into oblivion and I can be a super girly-girl who can properly pirouette and happens to also love punching people hard in the face. I feel great pride in being part of the conversation that compels girls to go up against boys, to help equal all the playing fields, to debunk the universal myth of the all-powerful male.

I want women who feel beaten down, at any stage of their lives, to read about my darkest moments and see that hope dies last. That there's always a way to get up, to find another avenue, to protect, to evade. I want women to own the fact that you can be pretty and a badass and graceful and gritty. You can be an athlete-warrior-dancer-ninja-cheerleader who can bake a cheese soufflé. You can be a tomboy in a tutu. You can wrestle and dance. You can wear high heels and lip gloss. You can do anything and everything. You can do it all. You can dictate your destiny.

People always ask me who I admire, who I want to be like. But the truth is that while I look up to lots of different people, I don't want to be the next anyone . . .

ACKNOWLEDGMENTS

I cannot express enough gratitude to my mom and dad. Mom, you have been my biggest fan and greatest supporter. You never lost faith in me through all my mistakes and successes. Dad, I am who I am because of you—a warrior with an attitude who won't take no for an answer. Thank you.

I'd also like to thank Ken Shamrock and Urijah Faber, for seeing my potential and nurturing my growth.

My story was not an easy one to tell; and now that it lives in the pages of this book, I'd like to also thank some of the people who helped make it happen: Margaret Stohl, Monica Haim, and Krishan Trotman—thanks for digging deep with me and helping bring my truth to life.

Finally, I would also like to express the deepest of gratitude to my managers Mark Schulman, Mike Roberts, Jeff Meyers, and Leah Almondia. You helped me rise from my ashes to become what I am today, and I am forever grateful.